Clément S

# How to fence Epee

The fantastic 4 method

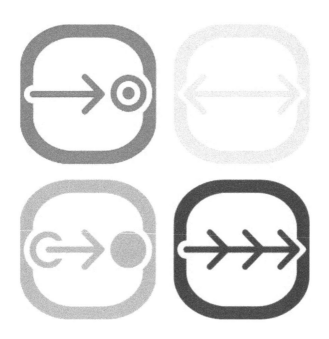

Translated from the French by Brendan Robertson

# How to Fence Epee

## The Fantastic 4 Method [1]

### - Clément SCHREPFER -

Translated from the French by Brendan Robertson

---

[1] Original title : "Faire de l'épée - La méthode des 4 fantastiques"

Edition : Books on Demand,

12/14 rond-Point des Champs-Elysées, 75008 Paris

Impression : BoD - Books on Demand, Norderstedt,

Allemagne

ISBN : 9782322011605

Dépot légal : November 2015

For Roland.

I hope that this method will help you progress in your pursuit of epee fencing, good luck! ☺

Clément

www.fairedelepee.fr / www.howtofenceepee.com - 2015

For Matt,

Thanks for your unwavering energy to train, learn, laugh, and compete with me! ☺

Brendan

# Preface

Quarte, sixte, septime, liement, redoublement, passata di sotto...fencing vocabulary that haunts all written works of our sport and feared by all but the truly initiated.

Every four years, for the French, fencing is a sport much discussed as a discipline that always earns medals (except London 2012)!!!

After London things changed in France. We tried to understand the reasons for the lack of success. Many who lived through this failure have undertaken personal initiatives to correct the mistake.

I believe this has helped Clément to embark on this writing adventure; to synthesize his personal vision of fencing and to share it to further our collective knowledge. We need this to democratize our sport, to make it more accessible and understandable to all.

All books on fencing focus on technique which is a very narrow focus for our sport.

This book looks at fencing in another way, from that of an enthusiast, a fencer who has lived in the world of fencing for over 20 years and who has acquired exceptional experience. Through this book you will be able to understand the real challenges faced by fencers of all levels. All fencers, from beginner to high level competitors, will find tools and tips in these pages to make real improvements.

The way in which Clément explains his vision of fencing, and in particular epee, is completely revolutionary! Until now, no one had made such a highly theoretical subject so accessible[1].

---

[1] It must be noted that most of the practical writings on fencing were written by former maîtres d'armes and date back more than 40 years.

The actors in the world of fencing are rarely unanimous when it comes to certain issues and this author's position will, hopefully, generate debate that will expand the vision of our sport.

This is possible because he explains fencing from the vantage of the athlete and not the educator. This is very important for us, the coaches and maîtres d'armes, to understand how athletes see our sport.

He breaks some myths but I'm a fan of this book because it summarizes the problems our current elite athletes face.

Throughout this book we discover stories, little "somethings extra", that are very useful and easily understandable by all. What's more, the use of logos for the Fantastic 4 is an innovative educational tool for this sport that I find very apposite.

I personally thank Clément for giving us the bounty of his experience and his thoughts about subjects that are important to all and to having presented us a new way to examine them.

Thank you for your innovative spirit and happy reading to all.

Hugues OBRY

# TRANSLATOR'S NOTE

Over my years of fencing I have had some wonderful maîtres d'armes starting with Zbignew Pietrusinski and, for the last 21 years my dear friend Jerzy Kajrenius. And recently, I have also had wonderful mentors such as maîtres Victor and Igor Gantsevich and Éric Boisse who have deepened my understanding of the game. These men have helped shaped me as both an athlete and a coach. For the last 19 years I have been living in my small home town of Vernon in the interior of British Columbia running my small team of eager athletes based out of the elementary school where I am a teacher.

Even as an athlete and a coach in a small town I have been able to maintain Shoshin, or the spirit of the beginner[1]. I am always looking to improve myself, to learn. When I am not learning from my coaches and mentors (who live, sadly, far away) I work closely with my training and coaching partner, Matt Clarke. I also scour the internet, I watch videos, and I buy and read books.

I read a lot of books.

This past year when surfing the net, I found a link to The Fantastic 4 book release. The colourful icons on the cover intrigued me, and since I read whatever I can, I got out my credit card and had one shipped over to Canada.

Once I started reading I couldn't put it down. The book is filled with the lessons I have learned over the years but, unlike learning fencing over more than two decades, and unlike any other fencing book I have ever read, this one codified it in a way and in one place that was easy to understand, easy to remember, and easier to put into practice (those colourful icons on the cover really help - trust me, I am a teacher). In short, it is the perfect book on epee fencing. As Hugues said, it's revolutionary.

I immediately started training my fencers through the paradigm of the Fantastic 4 and I quickly saw improvements. My athletes

---

[1] See the chapter on mental training.

have found it a boon as a way to think tactically when fencing and we have medals at major competitions to show for it.

It is a great way to teach tactics for epee fencing as you can differentiate your explanation depending on the level of experience of your fencers. I have been using it with beginner and seasoned fencers. I have the icons in my gym so that I can refer to them constantly and my athletes use them to explain their game plans and understanding of epee fencing through the paradigm of the Fantastic 4. All agree - it works!

Most of my fencers speak French but some do not. This was one of the impetuses to translate the Fantastic 4 to English. Another was to bring this excellent treatise on the epee to the masses as it deserves to be shared with all. I hope you find this method as fantastic as I have.

Happy reading!


Brendan Robertson

# CONTENTS

# Introduction

It has been 22 years since I discovered fencing and I have been competing just about as long. During these years I have trained from 2 to 6 times per week. I have not left my first club and have been under to tutelage of 8 different maîtres d'armes. I was able to fence at a high level and even had modest results[1]. Naturally, I went through ups and downs.

During all these years, I have been motivated to fence by my desire to improve, to learn more while having a good time with my friends in training and in competition.

Over the years, and more recently, I have come to realize that it is possible to explain fencing "in simple terms". I am not talking about explaining the rules, but rather to explain the fencing actions that have a positive effect (or not) and from this to derive a kind of "applicable concentration method" adapted to all fencing situations.

I can talk extensively with my training partners. But, to better help fencers who wish to improve (they know who they are), I had the idea of writing this manual to show in detail the totality of my understanding of how to fence epee. The result is in your hands. I will show you efficient solutions to real fencing problems through evidence-based examples.

Not that my purpose here is to tell my life story but it all began more than 10 years ago thanks to Laurent L. who, after seeing me lose miserably in the first round, gave me this good advice:

> *"It is obvious that you have some pretty good skills as a fencer but you just don't know what to do... You should write down your feelings when you are on your game and when you are not. Then, you can deduce a list of the*

---

[1] Team France for Juniors for the 2003 European Championships (then no. 8 in the FIE world ranking).

I thought I would give it a try. I never thought it would lead to such a broad conclusion as the one I will present to you below.

Of course, this is my vision of how to fence epee, and there are many others. I do not denigrate the importance of the elements or the more technical visions that show proper execution of technique, for many books already published show these better than I could. I therefore voluntarily skip this aspect of fencing to focus my discourse on this "new method/vision".

This new vision has the advantage of being adaptable to all fencing styles, because it is designed to bring out the best qualities of each individual fencer. It is an armature that forms the support on which you hang your technical and tactical skills. It allows you to progress in your understanding of the game by presenting, in a logical manner, the basic principles of good swordplay (and, by extension, of all individual combat sports).

Here I share my knowledge with no other pretension than to try to help you in your understanding of the mechanisms of efficiency (not performance) of epee fencing. I like to think that this vision is not far removed from the reality of the highest level of fencing and with this ensemble of knowledge you can be more effective and fulfilled in your practice.

Here is a distilled selection of advice that we "do not learn in school" (or we learn without really understanding the importance).

Before addressing the "Fantastic 4"—the condensed results of my "method" of fencing epee, I must explain the base on which it has been built.

---

[1] More or less. I don't remember it word for word...

Throughout my explanation, I add small "somethings extra" and at the end of each chapter I sum up the main points to remember so that my ideas are even more understandable.

Happy Reading!

# Chapter I: The Fundamentals

Throughout my explanation, I will endeavour to answer the simple question: "Why?"

Since we are not sheep and since it is always important to know what we are aiming to learn, even (and especially) in fencing, my approach will be explanatory and educational in its approach.

The idea is, in this first chapter, to look at the foundations on which the Fantastic 4 method is based. I will not over insist on these points, but they still have great importance for the application and understanding of this method. The basics: it's fundamental!

So, in this chapter we will discuss three basic aspects of good fencing:

- Technique
- Physical Training
- Mental Training

I do not mean by "basic" that these points are easy to learn and perform but that they must be part of your practice, so integrated that they become natural—to be a foundation on which to build, eventually, a more elaborate game with the Fantastic 4.

# I. TECHNIQUE

Technique in fencing? That's a lot to learn!

Technique is, since the beginning of the codification of sports, the essence of all sports. Fencing, quite obviously, has not escaped this rule. The evolution from duels to the modern sport of fencing has resulted in a multitude of specific movements whose principles and terminology are the foundation of the teaching of our sport.

"Quarte, sixte, lunge, retraite, tierce... "none of that here. These are words from our common fencing vocabulary and everyone can define it as they wish. However, to "speak the same language," I'll explain here what should be, in my opinion, part of your natural technical background in three points:

- En Garde Position
- Footwork
- The Strokes

## EN GARDE POSITION

It may seem awfully basic but a good en garde position is essential to perform the widest possible technical array.

What do I mean by "a good en garde position"?

- **Legs**: are to be flexed and balanced, while tilting the pelvis flat in order to stand straight.
- **Arm**: the hand should be in sixte, with shoulders relaxed while keeping the point in line.

Awfully basic you say? Indeed, all this seems obvious to seasoned fencers. But before we move on, and because otherwise it would just be too easy, let me explain why I find this so important.

### > flatten the pelvis and stand straight

What does this mean?

- Have both legs bent and try to tilt the pelvis[1] forward (which has the effect of "sitting" position).
- Engage your core muscles (abdominal and back).

WHY?

- Being balanced on our legs, we are able to easily go forward or backward.
- Having the back leg bent, we can better push forward to "jump" on our opponent (you cannot jump while standing, ed).
- By standing straight and "sitting" on our legs, the weapon arm/shoulder movements are freer, including "extending the hand" during arm extension.

Don't worry, we will explain these points throughout the book.

---

[1] The pelvic tilt is characterized by the "tucking in" of the butt.

## > Keep the hand in sixte with the arm bent and keep the point in line.

What does this mean?

- hold the hand in a slightly supinated position[1];
- have a relaxed shoulder;
- have the hand and point aligned towards the opponent
  - At the lowest: aim under the opponent's bell guard;
  - At the highest: aim at the weapon arm's shoulder.

It is important to keep the point of your weapon in this position without moving the hand. To not move the hand means that you must hold the same line as much as possible, **without reacting to your opponent's threats and false invitations** and to always know where the point of your weapon is aiming.

WHY?

- By remaining in line you reduce the distance to the target. Your point threatens your opponent by being on the lookout for scoring opportunities.
- By holding this hand position, we naturally protect ourselves and force the opponent to go around our guard (and thus make him lose his strong position).
- By having the weapon arm bent, one can extend and thus surprise the opponent (whereas a half-bent arm doesn't have the same element of surprise when attacking).
- In holding this position without reacting to threats, we mask our intentions and do not open our lines without reason. The surprise at the start of an attack may be more important.

---

[1] Supination is the rotation of the forearm that turns the palm of the hand towards the sky.

- Because moving the hand or not being in line, is to give your opponent information and possible opportunities to beat you. Your opponent will see your habits and reflexes and deduce your weak lines and know "how to attack".

Keeping your point high and straight at your opponent without aiming at his[1] hand, you will be threatening because your can move faster towards the target (between the chest and the shoulder of the weapon arm). It is a good sign if, when in this threatening position, your opponent constantly beats your blade. Your threatening position leads your opponent to focus on the wrong spot (we'll discuss this in the chapter about "target"). And, you can take the opportunity to surprise your opponent more easily.

You may argue that some fencers like to be in contact with the blade and this position will not bother them or will bother them very little. OK. Place your point under the bell guard to avoid your opponent's beats, then it will be up to him to "move", but stay in line to lose as little time as possible in the direction of the target.

I agree that these elements may seem natural for those who have fenced for years. If this is not the case, later in this book we will discuss tips to successfully hold your position.

---

[1] The translator wishes to note that the use of the male gender pronouns "he" and "his" is only used as a linguistic convenience and one can easily substitute "she" and "her".

# BALANCE

## > Stay balanced while en garde

Now that we know what to do with our legs and arms, we must now understand that it all goes together to stay balanced. Without the legs in proper position, the effort to have the arm available for moving efficiently will be increased.

The balance of the en garde position can be summed up as:

*"To release the weapon arm, bend the back leg"*

WHY?

- Because of mechanics!

When I am told to extend my arm, I make sure I perform a pelvic tilt and bend my back leg. This greater effort with the leg allows the weapon arm to be relaxed so it can extend easier.

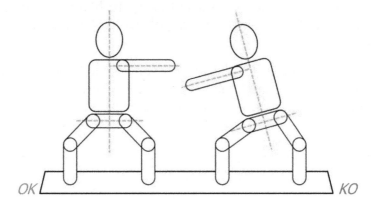

OK — KO

- On the left: a well-balanced position—the pelvis and the torso are straight = the arm free to extend easily.
- On the right: an unbalanced pelvis and the chest leaning forward = the arm lowers making a greater effort needed by the shoulder (or the torso) to extend the arm.

## THE DIFFICULTY

The back leg is usually at fault. A less bent leg (or an unbalanced pelvis) pushes the torso forward. This results in a loss of optimal en garde position and requires a greater effort from the shoulder. This leads to excess muscular tension which causes precision errors when attacking.

Having to compensate for the lower hand position with greater muscular effort (from the shoulder) we do not have the same accuracy when the arm is 100% available and dedicated to the speed and precision of movement.

The pelvic tilt is the best way to hold the en garde position and be balanced on the feet. The difficulty of keeping this position while moving is that we tend to "lift the buttocks" backward during a lunge. We must therefore consider the pelvic tilt, by "squeezing the buttocks".

This is especially important while lunging, where a pelvic imbalance pushes the torso forward (leaning) and the hand down.

## SOMETHING EXTRA

The pelvis is the pathway to remain straight. But we must also maintain a strong torso! When we think "core", we often think of the abs but what keeps you straight in the forward movement is mainly the back muscles.

So remember to strengthen your back muscles to complement your abdominal muscles.

# FOOTWORK

Now that you are in proper en garde, you must keep this posture when moving and keep the balance between sitting on your legs and keeping the arm available for extension.

What are the basic elements of fencing footwork?

- Forward
    - The advance
    - The jump forward
- Backwards
    - The retreat
    - The jump backward
- To carry out an attack
    - The half lunge
    - The lunge
    - The flèche

Again, all of this seems trivial, but I refer again to highlight the mechanisms and the mistakes often made when moving. And it is always worth doing things right.

Let's have a look:

- Disequilibrium
- Coordination
- Rhythm

## DISEQUILIBRIUM

Movement is created by the management of the disequilibrium. This is a mechanical fact - we put ourselves out of balance to move forward.

Beware, this is not the same "balance" as the balance of the en garde position!

Disequilibrium is when the center of gravity is located outside the support base[1]. Movement is created by "catching up" to this imbalance. It can be created by removing the support of the forward leg (and pushing with the back leg) but the balance of the pelvis and chest must be kept!

I feel like a drawing might help...

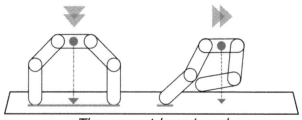

*The support base in red*

- On the left, the projection of the center of gravity is above the red zone. This is balanced.
- On the right, the center of gravity falls outside the support base, so it is out of balance. This imbalance creates a movement if we catch up to it. The pelvis meanwhile remains balanced.

The objective is to control this imbalanced movement, by removing one support or by the directional thrust of the other, or by both mechanisms simultaneously.

---

[1] Support Base: The polygon obtained by joining the various points by which a body lies on a plane. A body ceases to be in equilibrium when the vertical passing through its center of gravity falls outside of its support base (source Wikipedia).

Let us assume that to be effective while fencing, both forward and backwards movement must be executed quickly. Understanding this principle of balance, an effective solution to disequilibrium would be to shorten the time one is off-balance by leaving the floor for the least amount of time possible and alternating between front and rear supports - hopping, for example.

But hopping all the time from one support to the other, we risk tiring our muscles and losing elasticity and reactivity. It is a good idea but it's not a long term solution while fencing.

No, what matters above all is to **control the size of the movement**. Do not take large steps during preparations so as to leave the center of gravity close enough to the edge of the support base i.e. the polygon. Thus, you can create imbalance more easily in order to move forward or backward.

Conversely, taking too large a step forward does not allow you to easily change direction because of the size of the support base. The center of gravity is then at the center of too large an area to get out quickly and easily. The effort to make up for the possible movement from imbalance is more costly (and potentially longer).

Managing the "disequilibrium" of movement, means knowing how to have the legs available. Available to respond as quickly to the need to go forward as to the need to go backwards.

# COORDINATION

The famous arm-leg coordination! We have all heard "The arm first, then the legs."

I agree, but rather than "arm", we must say "point or tip first", always, it's **"the point before the legs"**!

And the point before the legs is valid going forward and backwards!

- advance during preparations with the point forward;
- when beating the opponents blade, it is with the point (without moving the hand) forward;
- when counter-attacking, it is the point first before retreating;
- when riposting after a parry, again it is the point before the legs.

## WHY?

Let's be clear, the objective of fencing is to touch without being touched.

### Legs before the point

If you advance towards your opponent without threat...you might as well let the opponent hit you directly; this is suicidal and counter-productive.

### The point before the legs

This is to threaten the opponent with the point without even advancing. In this case, we can say that: if you have to or want to advance, don't do it for nothing; this is a rational and efficient attitude.

I will discuss this idea in more detail in the "intentions" chapter.

In addition, by extending the arm, we move our center of gravity towards the edge of the support base; therefore it is easier to create a forward imbalance (to launch the attack, for example).

## RHYTHM

I have no theory about rhythm. It is unique to each person; it is adaptable to every opponent and can change even during a bout. It is part of the exchange and the power struggle that is created between opponents.

It is rhythm that one uses to defeat the opponent. It is therefore important to master it, to be comfortable in one's own rhythm and **have the ability to change** (to hold a more or less steady pace) without departing from the basics of what has been discussed up until now (to keep the en garde position in the proper place and to not open lines).

Changing rhythm during an action or during an exchange:

- During an action designed to surprise the opponent, start the action slowly (but threatening with the tip) and finish fast (the acceleration causes the surprise).
- During an exchange
  - to be able to accelerate your rhythm while your opponent keeps a steady pace.
  - Or the opposite: to slow things down and create a false rhythm to lull your opponent into slowness before attacking by surprise.

I will come back to this point in the putting into practice section of the chapter on "manipulation" (I promise).

# THE STROKES

Well, so far it has not been very technical, I grant. But do not expect too much more; I try, with this method (and in my regular practice), to think as little as possible about technique.

However, I will remind you that technique has an important place in the fundamentals and are seen here as concepts that you should not need to think about so much as they should be easy to execute.

I will not dwell on the considerable technical vocabulary of fencing. Many an author has already expounded on it with sufficient precision and talent. Here I group all technical moves in the term "strokes".

Anyway, we are now en garde properly and we can move efficiently. These two points will allow us to develop clean and precise technique, because this is, I think, what technique is about: **the proper execution of strokes**.


## FROM LEARNING TO EXECUTION

The ideal place to learn technique is during a private lesson. The maître d'armes passes on his knowledge and the correct execution. As such, this has the greatest influence on the technical development of a fencer.

However, a personal "technical vocabulary" will evolve according to one's own morphology, preferences, experiences, and physical abilities. It is then up to the fencing master to adapt and lead the student to further his art always with the main objective: the proper execution of the stroke.

While performing a technical stroke in fencing it is to be done **quickly, accurately, with good posture**, good position, and proper aim...

And it is valid:

- When moving;
- During preparations (feints, engagements, beats, opening lines, etc.);
- When attacking (straight thrust, disengagement, croisés, coupés, etc.);
- When defending (parries, retreats, counter-attacks...); etc.

What does this mean?

In each area, this implies rigor in the implementation of actions, both accuracy (arm) or motor (leg), based on an impeccable position (posture).

- For the en garde position and movement, it means be flexed, balanced, have a straight torso, and keep the point in line;
- For a beat, it means beat with the opponent's blade without moving the hand;
- For an engagement, it means start contact with the opponents blade with slight pressure with the foible (the "weak part" of the blade);
- For a parry, it means close the line from of the opponent's threat and deflect the opponent's blade.
- For an attack, it means ending the movement with the hand higher than the point and the torso straight.
- To bind an attack, it means engaging with the foible and change lines while advancing and maintaining contact with blade to switch from weak to strong. (see section below);
- For a coupé, it means start with the point in one line and finish the move sharply, so the point lands on target from the flex of the blade;
- ...and so on!

This accuracy is acquired through training, through repetition of the right moves, when learning the basics, during private lessons, during bouting... In short, through effort.


## THE SCIENCE OF THE BLADE

The blade is a "science" to successfully master so you can pass and place the point of the sword where and when you want despite the challenge of dealing with the opposing blade.

So, with a firm knowledge of this "science", you can deploy as much force with a French grip as with a pistol grip! It's only a matter of the **mechanics of movement**. You will learn the mechanics with your fencing coach. Here, I will present the key principles.

All becomes possible when you can comfortably use all parts of your weapon (foible/forte) with a firm grip and an understanding of the mechanics of levers.

The use of force is not necessarily enough. We must harness movement to move through more easily.

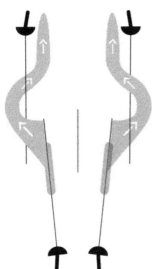

To take advantage of this mechanism, move the point before engaging the blades (point first—always). You must firmly hold your hand position: only the tip moves sideways. The blade does the rest. It will slide along the opponent's blade to deflect the tip.

In this example the opponent's blade is bound (by quarte on the left and by sixte on the right) by moving the point before advancing to the target.

Note that these examples work when attacking and when defending. But if you try these envelopments without movement, you cannot take advantage of the mechanics of the blade. This kind of action, subtle and precise, requires training and multiple repetitions. You must know where your point is, where your adversary's point is, and know how to intercept it.

Each of these movements is technical and could be explained on its own terms. But we are not here to learn all of them, refer to your fencing coach or other more academic writings.

We know that we are not robots and the perfect execution of all fencing movements during combat is a false hope.

However, poor execution of these actions would be unwise during bouting and would most likely result in a point for the opponent. It is therefore important to minimize errors. All the more so, **as the quality of fencing increases, the less room there is for imprecision**.


## HOW TO REDUCE ERRORS?

Errors can be reduced by doing nothing (yes, but not helpful) or by using a limited number of strokes that we have worked hard to master their execution perfectly. So much so that they would be the part of our game, our "best move", around which we could develop our game plan (although, wait and see what we can do with the Fantastic 4).

My point is this: work the execution of your strokes and identify your favorite actions, for the rest, we will see later how to put all of this together in competition.

Here is a small digression on the relationship between technical precision and the brain.

Note that any repetition of movement is recorded by neuronal connections. The repetition in training strengthens connections between neurons for this movement. They are then used to make it faster, more accurate, and more natural.

To train your neurons to make a move, close your eyes and visualise it (not during training). Repeat this exercise for several minutes. Your neurons are ready; you will improve the speed and accuracy of this movement.

In this context, the "fundamental[1]" exercises, often tedious, are still the best opportunity to work on our en garde position and our footwork, paying special attention to these important points:

- The bend in our legs (the back leg for sure)
- Managing balance (pelvis)
- Relaxing the shoulder
- Awareness of imbalance during movement
- Coordination
- Speed of execution

Don't balk at these exercises and apply yourself as much as possible, they are not called "fundamental" for nothing, they will help you land hits that would not land with poor posture and poorly controlled movements.

---

[1] Series of movements guided by the fencing coach.

Here is a brief summary of things to remember: technique.

1. The en garde position

- The weapon arm must stay in line;
- Both legs need to be well bent to serve as a base for the pelvis;
- Balance pelvis to hold the body upright.

2. Footwork

- Footwork needs to be small and the balance of the en garde position should be kept while moving;
- Whether to prepare an attack or defend, it is always the point of the weapon before the legs
- It is important to have the ability to change speed/rhythm during a match.

3. Strokes

- It must be an integral part of your game. Bladework must become as natural as breathing;
- Continuously work on perfect execution (no matter your level) to avoid "basic" mistakes in position, posture, and placement.

# 2. PHYSICAL TRAINING

Over the last 20 years, fencing has evolved considerably - especially in regards to the physical game.

The rise of emerging fencing countries and the professionalization of top fencers have resulted in athletes focusing on more scientific and efficient physical preparation. Increased competition has pushed the overall quality up and has also pushed nations to stream young athletes into specializing in one weapon increasingly early. This has resulted in young fencers beginning to specialize their training as well - modeled on the highest level.

Result: On the whole, contemporary fencing is more "professional" and more athletic[1].

I want to briefly look at the physical abilities necessary for the proper practice of the contemporary version of fencing. I will describe what capacities need to be developed to cope physically.

In most cases, the physical preparation is in addition to pure fencing training (general physical preparation and/or specific preparation). It then becomes a matter of athletes committing to investing time and effort to achieve goals. If one wants to move towards high performance, one must define priorities and be willing to pay the price required, because ultimately there are no free lunches.

It is not about developing your athleticism to the highest possible level but, as we are talking about competitive fencing, we can look at some simple improvements that will allow you to be better able to apply the Fantastic 4.

What are the ideal physical qualities for an epee fencer?

- Strength?
- Speed?

---

[1] For example, compare the Olympic finals of 1980s and those of the 2000s, the difference in physical effort is obvious.

- Endurance?
- Accuracy?
- Reflexes?
- Flexibility?
- Sight?
- Perception?
- Relaxation?
- All of the above?

Of course, being competent in all these domains would facilitate high performance, but how would one have the time and the means to train all of these qualities? And, given our different body types, how can one possibly develop all these qualities as an epee fencer?

It seems idealistic to me to think, "one must have all these aptitudes in order to be ~~good~~ effective[1]" And I'm sure we couldn't settle on just one. Especially since some of these abilities may be innate and incredibly difficult to acquire!

So let's focus on the most important ones that will make the difference during a bout:

- Endurance
- Explosiveness
- Relaxation

Would you have picked these three? I am not sure what most fencers would pick but I'll explain my choices.

Don't be concerned if these qualities are not part of your strengths, they are neither exclusive nor essential. My point is to present basic principles that explain, in my opinion, the physical mechanisms that can lead to effective practice, leading to better performance. But it is not necessary to be an athletic force of nature and these qualities can be learned[2], which is reassuring.

---

[1] I distinguish between efficacy (personal growth objectives) and performance (quantified and comparable sporting goals).
[2] This is true, regardless of your ability by varying intensities.

# ENDURANCE

Fencing, an endurance sport? Not really, but what I mean by "endurance" is the capacity to hold an effort longer than your opponent without wavering. From this point of view, yes, you have to have endurance.

The effort isn't purely "aerobic" like a marathon, but performed at "intervals".

## INTERVAL EFFORT

Interval effort is when you alternate full effort with more moderate effort or even downtime. In fencing, you must recover during downtime (between touches) to be physically ready for the next assault.

This seems logical, it goes without saying, and I agree. Fortunately, there are exercises that can help you recover during the bout.

Although this method was not intended to be a physical training manual, I'll just slip in a few exercises here and there.

### INTERVAL TRAINING

The goal is to vary the intensity of physical effort. Do so by running while alternating effort based on time. For example, for a session of about 30 minutes do:

- 3 sets 3 times:
    - 2 minutes jogging
    - 1 minute of fast running
- With a 5 minute break between each

The goal is to recover while jogging. You can vary the times according to your ability to hold intensive effort and still recover while jogging (for example : jogging 1 minute/30 seconds fast running or 2 minutes jogging/2 minutes fast running).

This exercise will increase your ability to recover quickly and it is perfectly suited to the effort required in fencing.

I want to clarify that this is not meant to replace regular endurance workouts or 20 to 45 minutes at consistent speeds to work at increasing your VO2max[1]. This "classical" jogging lets you know (and increase) your resilience to stress; to know your body in order to quickly identify the signs of fatigue during the bout is of paramount importance.

 *SOMETHING EXTRA*

<u>Shadow fencing</u>

Here is an exercise that I force myself to perform multiple times. It is simply to practice intense bout replicating footwork 3 times 3 minutes, alone, with 1 minute of rest between each period.

The 3 minutes are to be done without stopping the timer or the effort. Do not lunge/attack too often (5 maximum per 3 minutes), pay attention to your position, your speed, your preparations... See your opponent in your mind's eye to make the exercise more fun.

This "shadow fencing" is particularly suitable for interval effort training. I have always had good results from this practice.

---

[1] Maximal aerobic capacity.

# EXPLOSIVENESS

Muscular explosiveness is the ability for muscles to contract quickly and powerfully to develop the maximum force in minimum time. Coupled with good reaction time, the explosiveness will allow you to surprise your opponents with the speed of your movement. It will also change the rhythm of your actions: the famous "slow-fast" acceleration in motion.

With muscular explosion a fencer can "pounce" on scoring opportunities (for example).

Here too, through hard work, one can develop this ability!

If one accepts that movement is generated by the legs and that precision is generated by the weapon arm, we have two joint groups where explosiveness can be improved.

## PLYOMETRICS[1]

Do not panic, plyometric contraction is the most prevalent movement in sports, it is the most natural. Basically, plyometrics link an extension movement after a flexing movement.

Plyometric exercises double the ability to produce a more powerful movement over a very short period.

The principle is simple:

- Legs: when jumping from a height onto two feet, as soon as you touch ground you must quickly link the next hop with speed and explosiveness. Body weight is all that is needed, no load; to vary the degree of difficulty you only vary the height of the original jump.
- Arms: the perfect tool to improve explosiveness of arm extensions is the *medicine ball*[2]. Stand face to face with a partner, return the ball promptly upon receipt with both

---

[1] Source (French content) : http://entrainement-sportif.fr
[2] Heavy ball, weighing between 6 and 12 pounds.

hands. The muscles and joints of your arms will become more explosive.

The perfect way to improve power and increase the ability to react quickly is to work on specific muscles through circuit-training (hoops, studs, obstacles...) with some specific fencing movements. The circuit training can even be developed with interval effort training (by varying intensities every minute).

Be careful though, plyometrics can be traumatic if improperly performed or practiced too often. One session per week, in the form of circuit training and you will develop your explosive strength safely.

## SOMETHING EXTRA

We rarely think about it, but it is important to strengthen the back foot (+ ankle joint). Indeed, a weak foot (soft) cannot transmit a rapid forward thrust as effectively as a trained foot. Think of the foot like a fencing blade. A soft/weak blade will return to straight much less efficiently than a rigid blade.

How to do this? Simply by walking or taking small steps. With each step, roll the whole foot, from heel to toes. You will use and strengthen all the muscles of the foot arch.

# RELAXATION

How relaxation can help you make a difference in fencing? That's a good question and here are some answers.

Here, relaxation helps with the ability to isolate muscle movement. That is to say, to know how to move with efficiency. It helps one master the body in space and precision.

Fencing, by its very nature as a combat sport, creates muscle tension born of the fear of the fight. For beginners, this tension is typically manifested by holding the breath. To be able to be relaxed during a bout starts with knowing how to breathe at the rhythm of effort, to exhale when performing a stroke.

Being relaxed allows for efficiency in large movement (legs) and precise movement (weapon arm).

Again we are lucky as this too can be trained!

## PROPRIOCEPTION[1]

Proprioception is the ability to sense stimuli from within the body in regards to position, motion, and equilibrium. It is a result of internal feedback from joints, muscles and bones as well as sight and inner ear balance letting us know where each part of the body is and its movement relative to the rest of the body.

In competitive sport, proprioception allows one to make fine adjustments to movements and position in a variety of static and dynamic situations. And so, it can trigger, improve, and automate movement, whatever one's own position and that of the opponent.

---

[1] Source : http://www.e-s-c.fr and http://entrainement-sportif.fr (French content)

To exercise these sensors, one must practice stabilizing muscular micro-reflexes on joints that are unstable. In other words, exercise the body to perform a movement despite a general instability.

Specific exercises for fencing would be to put yourself in en garde and then stutter step quickly while advancing, retreating, and moving laterally. When you hear or see a sound or visual cue you are to start a specific action (step forward, retreat, jump, lunge, etc.) This exercise will help your body's ability to perform a specific movement regardless of your current position/balance. This will help your body to learn how to react quickly and efficiently during a bout.

Having control of your body through proprioception, you will be able to concentrate your efforts on relaxed efficient movement and avoid unhelpful muscular contractions while maintaining muscular precision.

On the whole: You want responsive legs while avoiding tension in the weapon arm. The goal is to be relaxed from the shoulder to be precise with the point.

What then is the balance between precision and strength seen in the hand grip and the shoulder?

Strengthening exercises for the shoulder girdle (shoulder, chest, triceps, etc.) and forearms should always favour explosiveness while avoiding the development of pure force. Of course, strength gives you the impression of being able to "power through"[1] more easily but it will inevitably be at the expense of speed, precision and explosiveness.

It would be counter-productive to hold the epee firmly and continuously. We must allow moments of relaxation in the shoulder and hand, precisely to successfully trigger explosive

---

[1] Rather than "powering through", consider using mechanical advantage by using the forte of your blade against the foible of your opponent.

muscle contraction (with speed and force) at the appropriate time.

In terms of training, do not unduly stress muscles. Work their plyometric ability. That is to say, perform rapid movements with moderate loads.

### Flexibility and Stretching

Logic dictates that flexibility can be a real plus in fencing. For example: hamstring flexibility helps lengthen lunges and suppleness of the shoulder allows for parrying during corps à corps, etc.

To gain flexibility, do not forget to stretch after fencing hard, in training and in competition. Stretching is not to be taken lightly. In addition to promoting muscle recovery and developing flexibility, they prevent the risk of painful joints tension.

It is important to note that particular strain on some of the muscles used in fencing (such as the iliopsoas) is directly related to the spine. Not stretching these muscles regularly can lead to acute back pain[1]!

---

[1] Having been a victim, I advise you to stretch!

Here is a brief summary of things to remember: Physical Training.

1. Endurance

- To have endurance in fencing is to be able to hold on longer than your opponent and knowing how to recover during interval effort.

2. Explosiveness

- Being explosive allows you to start any fencing action with power and speed.
- Plyometric exercises allows one to improve muscular explosiveness.

3. Relaxation

- Mastering your proprioception allows you to keep joints loose which allows for better point control.

# 3. MENTAL TRAINING

Those who know me will laugh at this point of the book.

This is actually one of my biggest weaknesses. Yet, I have been fortunate to be mentored (and sometimes even followed) by a mental coach who gave me the key to progress well in my approach to competition.

Anyway, even though I'm not a Zen master, I know what to do and how to think, at least in a basic way.

1. Training
   o Perseverence
2. Competition
   o Desire to Win
   o Before Competition
   o During Downtime

As you already know (but I insist on repeating), the mental aspect is a very important part in our sport. It has its place as one of the foundations of the practice of competitive fencing, as an equal to the technical and the physical aspects of the sport.

## PREAMBLE

The "Five Spirits of Budo[1] " teach us to be attentive to our state of mind, because they determine our actions in everyday life, and therefore our sport.

The fundamental states of mind of the "Way of the Warrior" are categorized as follows[2] :

---

[1] Philosophical basis of martial arts inherited from medieval techniques of warfare.
[2] Source (French content) : http://www.abiyr.be (Soke Pierre Champagne)

## SHOSHIN: THE SPIRIT OF THE BEGINNER

This is the spirit with which the beginner is prepared to receive his first teaching by the master. This mindset is essential to be able to assimilate knowledge and to progress. The practitioner who loses the beginner's mindset (by imagining he knows all) blocks progress.


## ZANSHIN: LINGERING MIND

It is a state of vigilance in order to cope with an event (an attack for example). This state of vigilance must exist before, during and after the action, in connection with the reactions of the opponent.


## MUSHIN: NO MIND

Mushin is a state of no (Mu) mind (Shin) in which the mind is fixed on nothing. In this state, the practitioner lets his thoughts pass without lingering. The mind remains unattached and free to react at any time. A mind that is set on an object or a thought becomes a prisoner. The mind fixed on thoughts does not work effectively. Mushin is reflected by "Mizu no Kokoro", meaning spirit (Kokoro) as water (Mizu). In other words, a mind that can flow freely like water.


## FUDOSHIN: IMMOVABLE MIND[1]

Fudoshin is the mind (Shin) imperturbable (Fudo). It is a mental state that no outside agency can come to trouble. This is the inner calm that allows one to cope, in the moment, in any situation. This concept of imperturbable spirit also corresponds to Mushin (a state of no thought).

---

[1] or "imperturbable"

Senshin is a mind (Shin) purified or enlightened (Sen) that transcends the first four spirits. It is a purified mind which will allow the practitioner to be in harmony with the universe (instead of being centered on itself).

The athlete must be able to analyze, understand, and control his states of mind in order to integrate them as assets when fencing. Without this effort on the mental aspect of the game, fencing can simply become physical training, instead of being an "ethical martial art," a source of progress for the individual.

These definitions show us the wisdom of ancient Japanese warriors. The philosophy presented here is quite applicable to the modern practice of fencing. Keeping them in mind, we will see them in the Fantastic 4.

---

## TRAINING

Training is the best place for lifelong learning. Keeping the "beginner's mindset", perseverance, and constant questioning pulls us towards the path of perfection, in three stages:

1. Simplification
   - Avoid unnecessary action/movement. They can give away our intentions to the opponent and are a waste of time and a source of fatigue;
2. Execution
   - A precise and mastered action is a well-executed action;
3. Efficiency
   - Adding the right power to an action; it would be futile to try to use force if we have not first mastered a simple and well executed action.

Training is the school for perseverance. Let's have a look.

# PERSEVERANCE

Why is it that we persevere? That even at the bottom, we still hope to rebound?

Passion? Pride? The desire not to disappoint (others and oneself)? Satisfaction of effort? The atmosphere? Madness? Teammates?

In fact, I do not know. What I know is that the most difficult training creates the best improvements.

When things are tough and we do not improve, motivation goes down and we do not want to make an effort, in short, when we are in a funk...well that's when we must persevere!!!

We must seek resources from wherever to work and stay strong, at the very least on the fundamentals of the game.

It will not be the most fun training but it certainly will not be a waste of time!

Progress is like an endless ladder where each rung represents a step towards mastery. Some rungs are difficult to climb. They appear impossible to us sometimes and we stagnate at the same level for a while. But through perseverance, and given time, to pass these same rungs again, they will seem more reachable or almost astonishingly easy.

## WHY?

Because, when we are physical and mentally not at our best, we must strive to stay effective and tough. Stay lucid even when under strain.

Remaining lucid, alert, when one is firing on all cylinders is relatively easy, but to remain lucid when the mind is not up to snuff is a challenge. This is why it is important to practice and persevere (you will know more about this concept in the "Patience" chapter).

It is in these moments that we gain in "energy resources" (see chapter with the same name).

Perseverance in training, bouting, lessons, in competition... this is how to develop toughness, and therefore gain the path to success. Go for it!

## SOMETHING EXTRA

### "The loser goes to 5" (exercise)

Here is an exercise to do during training to encourage perseverance during competition.

### First Part: defining roles

Fence normally to 5 point to determine who is the "winner" and the "loser".

### Second Part: complete your challenge

The second part begins when the winner gets to 5 and ends when the loser gets to 5. During this part, double touches don't count.

### The challenges

The "winner's" challenge is to end the game with the biggest gap possible. A good goal would be to double the number of touches by which you beat your opponent.

The "loser's" challenge is quickly finish to 5 points without letting your opponent score any more points. Ideally you would end the game at 5-5.

The advantage of this exercise is that it forces each opponent to work as carefully as possible to get single light touches. Even with very different ability levels, each fencer is challenged during the second phase of the game: persevere and hold on to complete the challenge.

It is fun, challenging, and useful to maintain a good fighting spirit even after losing the first part.

## DURING COMPETITION

To compete is to want to win.

Win a game, win a competition, win self-confidence... There are so many small victories to win on the road of progress. Competition is ideal for evaluating one's level and to glean these small victories. Get out of your comfort zone; it is about producing your best game, the great game!

We will see how to define the desire to win, prepare the approach to competitions, and discuss the management of downtime during competitions.

### THE DESIRE TO WIN

To win a game is to have at least one point more than the opponent at the end of regulation time.

Wow! That's new! You say sarcastically. I agree, but I also remind you that we are still in the chapter on the fundamentals.

One more touch, no matter the quality of its execution. At 14-14 in the final[1], the fencer that gets the hit will be the champion and the other becomes anonymous.

You have to do what it takes to get the last touch! Do not rush and make a bad decision, a poor preparation...

---

[1] And for each round of direct elimination and even each match!

Remove doubt and show the greatest determination with the intention of your touch. Of course, do not wait until 14-14 to have this "warrior" attitude!

Wanting to win is not improvised; it is a decision that is taken, resulting in a more or less aggressive attitude. We are talking about positive aggression, one that pushes us to find the physical and mental resources to outperform the opponent.

It is up to you to find your intrinsic motivation.

But, we are here to improve in a combat sport, so we must be better than the opponent to win (the point).

 *SOMETHING EXTRA*

### Nutrition

I'm not going to provide a course in nutrition. Here are just a few lines to make you aware that food is the fuel for your body! To keep going, you need the right fuel. Each person must find a suitable balanced diet. Eating healthy and natural is not a marketing fad; it's the balance that the body needs to keep moving[1].

So, avoid eating food with too much fat or too much sugar, especially for competition days. Sugar levels in the blood should be stable to ensure a constant supply of energy. Choose dry fruits to chocolate bars, whole grain items rather than hot dogs... Eat small portions at regular intervals. Your body will thank you and you will feel and see a real difference.

---

[1] For example, in his book "Serve to Win" Novak Djokovic describes his turning to "a gluten-free diet for perfect physical and mental health."

## ON POTENTIAL

Do not rely on your "potential", it is useless. I have often been in this situation... "Potentially I could have beaten everyone; if only I had paid more attention to my physical conditioning, if only I had not done this or that mistake, etcetera and blah blah blah[1]." Your ability is represented by your factual results; win your matches to show that you are the best. Whether you almost beat an opponent does not make you better, you still lost.

Be what you are doing and do what you want. In our case, what do we want? We want to improve and to win. Regardless of whether you could have done more, less, better or worse... do the best you can. Without "ifs" and without regret!

---

[1] With "if", we can do anything.

In music, rehearsals are training for the concert, where the artist has the most fun.

In sport, it's the same: we associate winning with pleasure. Where can you obtain the greatest victories if not in competition?

The answer is: **to compete is to have fun**[1]! To derive pleasure from the results of long hours of training, showing what we can do, achieving realistic targets, etc.

Why train? To improve? Why improve? To win? So, go for it: train, improve, win, have fun.

We often forget that it is about having fun. When we are serious in our training we get serious improvements.

### SOMETHING EXTRA

To be fit on an important competition day, it is important to be rested. Sleep well the night before the competition is good advice, I grant. But sleeping well two nights before the competition is even better!

For a Sunday competition, make sure you sleep well Friday and Saturday, for you will be all the better rested for competition.

It can be argued that "Sleeping is life" on the assumption that if one sleeps badly, we live badly. This applies perfectly here.

---

[1] QED

# DOWNTIME DURING COMPETITIONS

Once we have registered for a competition, we may be anticipating and looking forward to fencing. What we don't think about at this stage is the between match waiting during a competition. This downtime during competitions is real and you have to manage it.

From registration to the finals fencing tournaments take several hours. It is inconceivable to be able to keep the same level of concentration during this long period. This brings up the notion of "interval concentration."

In order to have moments of relaxation between matches it comes down to finding a ritual to "restart". After downtime you want to have the ability to restart each new match with the clearest mind possible. This is an ability you must have to improve results when competing.

## WHY?

The spirit guides our actions. It is counterproductive to tire our mind during downtime. It prevents us from using our physical resources in the best possible way. We shall discuss further in the "energy resources" section.

It comes down to identifying the amount of concentration necessary at different times during competition:

| Phase/Length | Level of concentration |
|---|---|
| Arrival at competition - about 1 hour before the start | No need for mental effort here. Just know that you will soon need to change gears. |

| General warm up ~ 30 to 45 minutes before the start of poules | Your body gradually warms up. Do the same with your mind. Slowly begin to sharpen you focus up to your first poule bout.[1] |
| --- | --- |
| Depending on the size of your poule the time between matches can vary from 1-4 bouts. | Ramp up to full concentration for each bout while ignoring the results of completed matches. Every bout is a new event that deserves your mind to be clear and alert. |
| The first DE bout[2] - this can be up to one hour after poules. | This can be seen as a fresh start. You have had time to get some downtime and are ready to re-enter the competition afresh. |
| Second DE match - from 10 minutes to one hour wait. | Whatever the wait time, organize your downtime through the phases of, decompression, re-focus, ready. |
| Etc. | The re-focus time varies for each person: from "instant" to several minutes with the need for a preparation ritual. Learn to master your own needs. |

The objective is to arrive at the beginning of each match with calm, ready to fight by giving your all technically, physically, and mentally.

---

[1] We shall see soon how this looks light of the Fantastic 4.
[2] Direct Elimination bout

Having our equipment in perfect working order is paramount for competitions.

There is nothing worse than having your mind preoccupied with equipment issues. Illegal point, too soft a blade or with an s-curve, a loose grip, a broken strap, a bent mask mesh, or socks that fall...

Whatever the problem, it will prevent us from giving our full concentration in the match and will potentially be an "excuse" (inadmissible) for poor performance.

Do not allow equipment problems. Always have at least 2 identical and well maintained swords.

## → WHAT TO REMEMBER

Here is a brief summary of things to remember: Mental Training.

1. In training

- Through rigorous training, what seems impossible is actually within our reach (think of the rungs of the ladder).
- Rome was not built in a day. Train regularly and persevere in difficult times and you will progress naturally.

2. In competition

- The desire to win is the essence of combat sport, do not lose sight of this.
- Competitions are a place to have fun; apply new learning, show new skills, give your best... to win.
- Manage your concentration levels based on the flow of the event. This will help you to have the energy needed for each new confrontation.

# Chapter 2 : The Fantastic 4

Here we go!

With these basics covered and assuming that you adhere to them properly, we can now talk specifically about the "Fantastic Four"!

## WHAT ARE THEY ABOUT?

As I mentioned in the introduction, it all started just over 10 years ago. I started to make note of my feelings when I was fencing well and I came up with a list of important fencing concepts that I could concentrate on.

Initially, the list was long. I tried to think of all the concepts by dictating them to myself before matches. It looked like this:

- Hand to the right[1]
- Point in line
- Bend my back leg
- Don't follow the hand
- Don't stop moving
- Fight for win
- "I decide"
- Be "wicked" on the target
- Relax the shoulder
- ...and so on!

---

[1] Because I am right handed.

It was way too long. It was not possible to think of ALL these things before each game without missing one.

This is especially true as the ability to concentrate diminishes with physical energy (and vice versa). We'll see about that later.

So I gradually reduced this list. Not by eliminating points, but by grouping, testing new lists, finding new points, new groups, etc. I sometimes forgot to use it and fenced only by instinct, by being in the moment.

And finally, as always, to understand what was happening, why this or that action worked (or not), I returned to this analysis and concentration method.

After 5 years of testing, more or less rigorously, here is the final distilled list to know the "why" and understand the "how"; the core of epee fencing: "**The Fantastic 4**".

Let us review them one by one before observing how they integrate as a whole when put to practice.


## WHY ARE THEY FANTASTITC ?

Without revolutionizing your knowledge of fencing because they are nothing more extraordinary than the "fundamentals" as we have just seen, they are much more important in the sense that each touch scored can be explained by one of these four points. They can summarize all the mistakes made at the highest level, no less!

*"Why am I not the world champion?"* [1]

Because the constant, rigorous, and effective application of this method is complex! And there is "theory" and "practice"; the best fencing masters are not necessarily the best fencers, right?

---

[1] Good question. ☺

As for me, I can objectively admit that my life choices and my personal investment did not lead me to performance at the highest level[1]. In addition, as crazy as it sounds, I've never managed to fence an entire competition with this method without faltering somewhere[2]. One day perhaps, you never know...

However, in recent years, it has allowed me to understand my sport and gain a real sense of calm control of what can happen on the piste. The constant questioning it implies also allows me to continue to learn and progress after more than 20 years of fencing.

You will notice that the basis of this reflection **does not concern itself with technical action** such as: "when I feint a straight thrust with disengage with step and lunge, it works well" or "I'm going to take the blade in quarte-octave bind." And that's why it can be potentially used by all types of fencing styles, because it is not based on specific technical abilities but on tactical points, on concentration, on analysis and on attitude.

To allow for all possibilities of action and reaction, we have seen in the "Five Spirits of Budo" that **we must not limit our mind by locking onto a game plan of "strokes"** in which the touches are only made in order to achieve a "technical stroke".

For example, in my approach:

*"I'll make a beat quarte-sixte croisé"*

Although the purpose of this move seems to be to hit the opponent, this sentence is the great "anything".

---

[1] Focusing my energy on my education, music, and other creative projects, I was not ready to "pay the price" necessary to become a champion.
[2] The basics (physical or mental) often find me lacking.

Of course, I do not exclude that we can have favorite "moves". Moves that are developed through practice, that are related to our morphology and our reflexes. And we always enjoy when we score a point using them. But we shouldn't build our game plan around them. Focusing our attention on achieving a single gesture (stroke) significantly reduces the range of possibilities.

Everyone has heard that the important thing is not the destination but the journey. Transposing this to fencing—it doesn't matter how we technically score a touch. If the point was made, it is thanks to preparation, observation, and the construction of an error by the opponent and the ability to seize the opportunity created.

With this method, I hope to convince you by giving you food for thought, the tools and the advice necessary to open the "field of possibilities". While keeping in mind the ultimate purpose of fencing: touch without being touched.

So take the Fantastic Four as a method (among others) as a basis to progress in your learning and go further in the understanding of epee fencing.

Point number one: **look at the target.**

## WHAT DOES THIS MEAN?

It means **fix your attention on the target.**

Here, the term "target", the single point on all opponents between the shoulder and the chest (weapon side). Focus your attention on the target and develop your peripheral vision to be on the lookout for opportunities that arise in the observation of your opponent.

Regardless of the position and movement of the opponent's hand, your attention should always be on the "target"

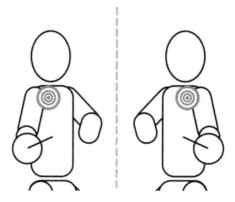

*Right hander*                                   *Left hander*

Even before you go en garde, you can already look at the target and start for focus on it. The most common mistake is to focus attention on the weapon hand or the weapon point. This is actually a mistake because all opponents will have a different hand game. Some are left-handed, some are right-handed. Some search and some avoid the blade. Some hold the hand high and some hold the hand low. You will find some in line or off-centre, moving or stationary, with more or less elongated arm, etc. All these possibilities do not allow us to have a consistent and efficient game plan.

To follow the opponent's hand, is to be exposed to uncertainties. When in fact, we always know where it is. There is no need to look at it to threaten it or touch it.

The idea is to focus on a fixed point, a less moving point, a point on the torso.

## HOW TO KNOW IF IT'S GOOD?

During a bout there are some signs that let us know that we are not focused on the target.

One must be focused on the target and paying attention to peripheral vision. If we follow the weapon hand too much, our actions will be too large, and we will make mistakes in distance, etc.

To illustrate my point, here are examples of the risk posed by focusing too much attention to your opponent's hand.

*The risk of changing your en garde position:*

If you seek to align yourself on the opponent's hand you will offer an open line of attack for your opponent.

*The risk of _point inaccuracy_:*

The opponent's hand will move faster than his target (sixte), we cannot follow it and still be accurate (by moving the hand, precision is lost).

*The risk of _misjudgment of distance_:*

Fencing distance based on the hand is not viable, it moves too much and arm length is different between opponents (The real distance between us and the adversary is the distance between the centers of gravity between each fencer's feet. And above the feet is the target. We must therefore base fencing distance from the target, more on this later).

*The risk of _responding too often to threats_:*

The threat comes from the point of the weapon. By watching the hand we are subject to too many adverse feints (and therefore we react too quickly and we show openings).

*The risk of _holding back_:*

If you look at the hand as target against a fencer who makes a lot of blade contact you may be intimidated for fear of having your blade taken by the opponent. Then we might not dare to attack.

---

## TARGET VS. OPPORTUNITIES

Warning: **looking at the target does not mean only touching the target**! Distinguish between target and "opportunities".

Peripheral vision should allow you to stay focused on the target (without following the hand) and to be attentive to error signals from your opponent.

The signals:

- Opening of lines :
    - Wrong en garde position;
    - Searching for the blade.
- Movement without intention:
    - No direct threat.
- Wrong distance:
    - Opponent moves into direct touch distance
    - difficulty following the imposed rhythm;

These errors caused by the change in our preparations are opportunities to be seized to build an action leading to scoring a touch.

So, the close targets (hand, foot, thigh) are not to seen as targets but as opportunities that would be openings in the en garde position or the footwork of the opponent as a result of our threatening preparations[1].

Logically :

- We do not choose to touch the foot or thigh as first intention: we go for the foot if the opportunity arises in combat, when we have managed to get our opponent in a high line while being in range for this attack.
- We do not choose to touch the hand without reason: we will go to the hand if the opportunity arises in combat, when we managed to open the opponent's en garde position.

These small details would have been observed with peripheral vision without showing our intentions to the opponent (en garde position maintained while looking straight at the target).

This "fantastic" is a way to improve one's game and the potential of possible reactions when faced with adversity so as to not react

---

[1] Although, the opponent may just open these lines without provocation if you are patient.

to just any hand movement and not be locked into carrying out specific technical strokes.

How to get your opponent to make the mistake of looking at your hand?

Try to disrupt his concentration by moving your point, by shifting your hand or from contact with his blade. Because of the constant disruption of his position, he will necessarily pay more attention to your hand.

But keep in mind that **creating errors and openings in your adversary's game is done primarily with legs** (with footwork we can lower his attention through fatigue) and not with the hand (which would risk opening your own lines or making en garde position errors).

Here is a brief summary of things to remember: The Target.

1.  Don't look at the hand
    *   Disregard the hand as a target and focus on sixte. This will allow you not to be bothered by the blade and to judge distance on just one spot that moves much less.

2.  Make the distinction between target and opportunities
    *   Be on the lookout for opportunities without fixing your attention on these targets (other than the target between the shoulder and the heart, of course).

# 2. DISTANCE

*Point number two*: **Be at the right distance.**

## WHAT DOES IT MEAN?

It means being at the distance that puts you **beyond the direct reach of the opponent** while being close enough that you can **easily threaten** your opponent with your point without having to get too close.

→ Distance: The space that must be crossed to score a touch, which is filled to by the size of your attack.

It varies according to the "size of the attack": yours and your opponent's, of course. Since most attacks don't have the same length, it is necessary to **constantly change the length of the space between you and your opponent** to hamper his ability to assess distance. You will be able to control the distance and decide when you will enter into the direct reach of your opponent in order to attack or provoke an attack.

By this definition, the right distance constantly changes during the match and is different for different opponents. One must be able to change the distance to deal with different types of fencing styles, to score touches in different ways.

We often hear that we must "play with distance", make the opponent fall short, "break the distance", etc.

The idea is to play with distances; **to vary distances** by moving in and out of your direct touch distance and that of your opponent.

## HOW DO YOU KNOW IF IT IS GOOD?

There are signs that help you know when you are too close:

- Being hit on your advanced targets (hand, foot, or thigh) from just being en garde
- Being hit by an attack started without rhythm, on the spot

They are unconditional signals! > You have to be farther away so as to be "**out of direct reach**."

Farther back, but not too far; you must accept to be under threat, by learning not to react in just any way or to every threat (hence the importance of not focusing on the weapon hand).

To threaten means to make the opponent react with the point of your weapon (referred to the section on "Intention").

### SOME PROBLEMS YOU MIGHT ENCOUNTER

#### The opponent is taller than me

Nothing new here: stay out of direct reach and use distance so you can decide when you can threaten. Take care not to make your preparations too large or you will get stuck on your legs, use your "small stature" to be quicker on your feet.

#### The opponent is walking all over you

I cannot get myself out of direct reach of my opponent.

Backing up is good but the piste does have an end. If he chases you down the piste it is because he doesn't feel any threat when close to you and he is trying to provoke you to attack. Refuse to give ground too easily but keep distance far enough so you are still out of harm's way.

To not just back up, you must remain threatening and hold your ground. One idea would be to hit him hard so that he understands there is a real threat if he continues to advance. It is risky, I grant, but it is better than letting someone walk all over you.

## The opponent is always out of distance.

I can't seem to threaten him.

We must succeed in pushing him to the end of the piste where he can no longer retreat to be out of harm's way. This is not easy because nobody backs up easily but it is a risk to take or else we fall short in our attack because we can't cross the distance to hit.

## USE THE PISTE

It's like all combat sports—we must "lead" the opponent all over the field of play in order to disrupt, to deceive, to score points. Use the piste:

- in length
- in width

## IN LENGTH

Using the length of the piste in the preparation of an attack allows you to attack in different ways depending on where one is on the piste.

### WHY?

Why not start attacks in the middle of the piste?

Because it leaves too many options for your opponent. He would have plenty of time to:

- Back up (move far from danger)
- Attack (close the distance)
- Parry

Scoring actions are often made in the centre zone of the piste.

- Sometimes because both fencers refuse to back up.
- Sometimes because a fencer has decided to attack at the first available opportunity.
- Sometimes the fencer's strategy is based on performing specific strokes.
- Too often it is all of these reasons combined.

These small mistakes reveal a lack of patience in the preparation of the attack or show a lack of use of the length of the piste.

We are talking about "changing tactics" depending on where we are on the piste. Indeed, we need to know if we are on our side of the piste to keep distance or to draw them forward. Both cases involve a different attitude vis-à-vis the management of opportunities and threats.

By bringing the adversary onto our side, we know our position in regards to the end of the piste and we can give the impression of being "in danger". Being here on purpose, there is no fear, we can vary (always) our reactions depending on incoming threats.

Conversely, when on the opponent's side of the piste we must intelligently push and pressure. First we must push him to the end of his piste so that he can no longer retreat (that's one less solution), and then find a scoring opportunity by using various threats.

Regardless of what side of the piste we are on, and whether we are leading or following, there are two aspects to prepare:

1. Move the fight into one area of the piste;
2. Manage the threats and opportunities depending on the area.

## IN WIDTH

Not only do you have to use the length of the piste when creating opportunities for scoring touches, you have **the width of the piste that also allows for many scoring possibilities** (or mitigate those of the opponent).

It is therefore important to position oneself laterally depending on your game plan and the intentions of the adversary: face him, always.

## RIGHT-HANDED VS. RIGHT HANDED (OR LEFT-HANDED VS. LEFT-HANDED)

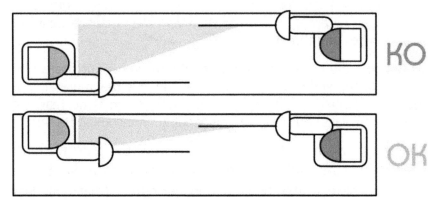

KO: fencing in the middle or on the right side of the piste, offset from the opponent = we give him a large angle of attack.

OK: fencing on the left of the piste, face to face, to reduce the angle of attack in order to limit his possibilities.

## LEFT-HANDED VS. RIGHT-HANDED

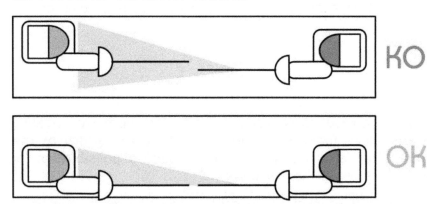

KO : fencing in the middle of the piste or the left side = we give him the possibility to attack from both sides.

OK : fencing on the right side of the piste reduces the angle of action in order to limit his possibilities

An opponent ostensibly seeking to touch the inside of the hand (right-hander/right-hander or left-hander/left-hander) should fence directly in front of the opponent on the "inside" of the piste to reduce the angle (Ex 1 in the diagram above)

An opponent trying to touch the outside of the hand (right-hander/left-hander) should fence directly in front of the opponent on the "outside" of the piste to close the outside line (Ex 2 in the above diagram).

If the opponent fences in the middle of the piste in a very linear fashion, we can shift to one side to disrupt the action or make him believe you have a line open for attack.

You may be thinking:

*"Yes, but this will also affect me by reducing my angle of attack!"*

I would respond by saying that, in fact, the angle is always a straight line forward.

The "Science of the Blade" says: to be in a strong position, is to offer the forte of his blade in the initial en garde position. Thus, no line appears open and maintaining this unwavering en garde position, we provoke our opponent to circumvent or move the blade. The opponent will have to go around or beat the blade and when he tries, he will not be doing so from a strong position. When he changes his line to beat or circumvent our blade he is making a possible mistake so we can more easily[1] score if we can seize the opportunity.

---

[1] And when we stay en garde in line, as we have seen, we maintain the shortest distance to the target.

Here is a brief summary of things to remember: distance.

1. Control the distance
   - Seek to impose fighting distance and refuse to fence under direct threat of the opponent.
   - Voluntarily vary distances to disrupt the opponent in his perception of the game.
2. Use the whole piste
   - Use the entire piste, both in length and in width to vary the types of preparations.

*Point number three*: **Be Patient.**

## WHAT DOES THAT MEAN?

This means you must start your actions **only when you have made a conscious decision to do so** when you have successfully stayed focused longer than your opponent **to punish him for his mistakes.**

This is, in my opinion, one of the most important points[1].

→ Being patient is not "waiting until something happens." It is successfully mastering energy resources **to remain lucid during the effort of fencing** to not start your scoring attack until you decide after creating the error in the opponent's game.

Understand here that physical and mental resources are inextricably linked. The objective of this fantastic is to remain lucid longer than your opponent, hence the concept of "patience".

To be lucid for a long period of time, it is important that the physical investment of fencing does not take too much away from

---

[1] Which, along with "intentions", would form a sort of "ultimate fantastic."

mental energy. Otherwise your focus drops and you lose concentration.

To be patient, we must be in good physical shape and know how to use it wisely. It is not about crushing the opponent physically rather to have the energy to be able to exhaust him mentally and be "present" to punish his eventual mistake (movement, distance, concentration, intention...).


## HOW DO YOU KNOW IF IT IS GOOD?

In general, we are able to pay attention during 30 and 50 seconds of effort. All touches born of an exchange of less than 30 seconds are therefore theoretically a bit rushed. That does not mean that we should do nothing for 45 seconds and attack at once, or that we should not take advantage of an opponent's error occurring before 30 seconds has passed.

But we must first lower the opponent's concentration. We must succeed in wearing him out by:

- physically by leading the pace and movements;
- mentally by threatening the opponent in several areas (varying targets and distances);
- tactically by manipulating and diverting his concentration (feinting parries, beats in all lines)

Worn out and weakened, the opponent will launch something through fatigue (physical or mental). He will have lost patience.

## EXERCISE (FOR TRAINING)

During training bouts do not attack before the opponent. Wear down your opponent while waiting to see when the opponent will start his attack. Thus:

- If he surprises and hits you it means that you lost your focus before him;
- If, despite your intention, you launch first, it means your physical resources were not his equal;
- If you succeed, it is that you had more physical resources and were more lucid than him, and, therefore more patient.

This can also be a way to approach a competitive match in order to gauge the opponent's resilience in the early exchanges of a bout.

It is crucial to build scoring touches through patience. An exchange that lasts more than a minute is physically demanding. The fencer who scores a touch was able to be more lucid (or keen) than the other by not attacking in any way or at any time. For the subsequent hits, the opponent will try to take less time (because he's tired), so it is up to us to be physically and mentally fit enough to further punish and launch at the optimal time, only when we decide.

*"Decide, launch, go... What is involved?"*

Good question. We are talking about the actions that lead to scoring a hit; the attack that will end the exchange. The point is to not to engage by "default" or by "fatigue", because the opponent has managed to make us attack, but in having really chosen the time and manner. You see?

The idea is to find the moment when the solution will be most accessible, offered by a lack of focus in our opponent. For this, it is sometimes necessary to refrain from attacking, even if it means feeling a somewhat positive "frustration". Being patient, also means letting possible scoring opportunities pass by without chasing them down and keeping focus until THE right opportunity comes.

Patience, the mother of all virtues, is also true on a fencing piste!

## ENERGY RESOURCES

This diagram explains the link between mental and physical resources. Together they form a "whole" energy.

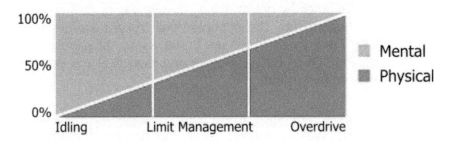

The trouble is that while the mental and the physical are inseparable, there comes a time when focusing on one sacrifices the other.

It comes down to knowing how to control one's energy capacity to not go into the red zone, into "overdrive".

## IDLING

While "idling" physical effort expenditure is under control. The ability to concentrate is high. If this level of effort is sufficient to handle fencing distance, one is at liberty to do well. The more we are at "ease" physically (no need to invest too much effort), the greater the mental reservation available. This is how we would like to start each match. But as any bout progresses the physical effort needed increases; one must try to stay in the "idling" zone in order to maintain our ability to concentrate.

## LIMIT MANAGEMENT

"Limit management" is the part of a bout when one has to remain lucid despite physical effort. It is a balance to control. You must not to tip the scales the wrong way and choose fencing actions through "fatigue" rather than "by choice". It is important to know your physical limit to learn to judge the intensity one must use when fencing. When you feel yourself beginning to unravel, do not hesitate to "disengage" out of distance during the exchange to catch your breath (and your mind) between touches.

## OVERDRIVE

By "over-reving", physical investment encroaches on our ability to concentrate. We go "into the red" and the risk of losing lucidity is greater.

To lose lucidity is to lose:

- point accuracy and movement control;
- the ability to analyse distance and strategy;
- the ability to maintain self-control by risking negative emotions and even nervousness.

The only solution is to lower the physical intensity of the match to pull oneself together (by retreating after close contact, maintain greater fencing distance, slow down the pace, ...). **The goal is to get our opponent into this difficulty before us**, without even entering.

Training can increase our energy resources in both areas. During individual lessons, for example, you can train to go "into the red" while maintaining as high a concentration level as possible to perform the exercises correctly with technical precision, so we better learn our physical limits. **Being "in shape" therefore helps to keep our mental edge** (in lucidity and concentration).

*And conversely*

I also draw your attention to the fact that this can also be read the other way. Somewhat less common or systematic but very real is when the mental resources take precedence over physical resources.

This is the case when we mismanage downtime in competition, for example. When we wear down our mental resources by using them at the wrong time, we start the problem in the wrong direction, leaving less room for physical resources to be expressed.

Being "paralyzed" by stress and the desire to do well has actually happened to me more than once. As my concentration hyper-focused on this, my physical abilities were not able to express themselves. I was "in the green" mentally, but physically exhausted from too much energy taken up by my mental resource. Of course, this is not good. We must succeed in managing moments of concentration and then move to downtime to optimize our energy resources. (see the Something Extra "Sleep is life").

Here is a brief summary of things to remember: Patience

1. Decide when to go
   - Manage to hold back until the opportune time, by choice, not by the reacting to the opponent's preparations.
2. Know your capabilities
   - Manage your energy resources so as to not yield to physical and mental fatigue (or "attrition").

*Point number four*[1]: **no forward action without intention**.

## WHAT DOES IT MEAN?

It means that **any forward movement of your legs or your weapon point must have at least one of the following three intentions**[2]:

- make act
- make react
- or to score a touch

Here is the most important point to me.

## WHY?

The step is not a trivial movement—it is to go forward. And going forward is to approach or enter into the direct touch zone of the opponent.

We do not go into the lion's den without knowing what to do when there.

---

[1] *Last but not least*
[2] Hence the three arrows in the blue icon

Thus, regardless of the opponent's reaction, it will be caused by our conscious decision and we will already be prepared to respond in a constructive way.

Beware, it does not mean that we must move forward or backward all the time. We are not talking of movement but of intentional attitude, with the advancement of the point.

Before continuing, I included this small point to be sure we are talking about the same thing.

- To defend is to avoid a threat. This can be done with the legs backwards or with the blade by parrying.
- To attack means to threaten. This can only really be done with the point of the sword[1] (see "the point before the legs" in the fundamentals).

Moving forward has to be done carefully. We must manipulate the opponent into making an error, we must provoke it. It is not constructive to wait for the opponent to make a mistake and in doing so we risk being hit by an opponent who catches us by surprise. We should have provoked the attack to control it.

Our preparations can help us know the different types of actions possible to undertake. It is therefore necessary to give meaning to each preparation; to leave as little room as possible for chance and indecision.

→ Create your game while measuring the risk.

Remember

We have agreed that:

- **we focus our attention** on all opportunities (started by the opponent/provoked during the exchange) > target.

---

[1] It is very important to master the point-leg coordination (see Fundamentals n°2) to succeed in threatening in the most effective way possible.

- **we master the distance** (between being out of direct reach and within the possibility of threatening with the point) > distance.
- **we decide to start an action** (after first lowering the opponent's concentration) > patience.

→ With these first three principles understood, we are now ready to **create our game in all areas** by choosing our forward preparations.

## HOW TO PREPARE A HIT?

Our intentional forward movements represent all the preparation work during the exchange. It is these, interspersed with more relaxed moments to "drown the fish"[1] with movement (and to breath a bit), which will allow us to discover where are our opponent's weaknesses, by observing his reactions and the openings in his lines.

There are many kinds of preparations:

- Threats with the point;
- Intimidation by intensity variation in rhythm;
- Invitations through false openings of line or slowing of pace;
- Blade provocations (engagements or beats).

We must then observe our opponent's reactions to our choice of preparations. "This one to provoke an attack, this one to illicit a certain reaction, or finally, this one to score a touch if an opportunity arises during the exchange."

---

[1] Translator's note: in the original French version of this book the French expression "noyer le poisson" is used here - literally "drown the fish. However, there is more to this expression. As you can guess, it comes from fishing. When you have a fish hooked you need to tire it out before you land it. In order to tire it, you pull (until its head comes out of the water - in essence to slowly drown it) and let go, pull and let go, over and over. The fish will be confused and tired and you will land it. This analogy fits fencing. You press and release your opponent to tire and confuse to make it easier to score.

However, this does not mean to do preparations all the time (be patient), at the risk of "falling apart" showing our intentions to the opponent too much and create our own downfall. To not fall apart, it is important to remain strict on the fundamentals: hold the en garde position. And don't show your intentions by varying your preparations.

During the match, the goal is to be on the lookout for opportunities by varying the different types of preparations, always with intention and good distance, while also allowing time for the opponent to show the weaknesses and openings in his preparations.

So let us focus on the intention of our own forward actions to limit our mistakes.

## SOMETHING EXTRA

"Can we go backward without intention?"

I want to say "Do whatever you want when retreating!" but retreating, how does that help?

- Retreating opens the distance
- It avoids a threat by removing oneself from direct hit distance.
- It can make the opponent advance to control the distance

This third point offers a new perspective: retreating can be used for the construction of a deliberate (with intention) attack!

To test: Risk taking is minimal as we move away from the opponent but by varying the size of steps we can "close the distance" (who would have thought?) to get the opponent into our direct hit distance and carry out an attack.

Of course this can only work if the opponent follows us forward without intention, because he may have lost his lucidity.

But, back on topic: <u>No forward action without intention</u>.

## MAKE ACT

By feinting a distance mistake or opening a line to get your opponent to attack, we are trying to make him believe that our preparation is not a threat and that it is possible to attack.

As we prepared for it, and that our preparation is not too big, we can react in several ways:

- by backing out of danger so his attack falls short
  - o and acting then, for example by:
    - retreating + counter-attacking
    - retreating + parry-riposting
    - retreating + flèching
  - o doing nothing to drown the fish
- by making a direct counter-attack
- by creating a counter-time in the attack
- by parrying his attack

### FEINTING ERRORS

Feinting distance mistakes can also be made only with the arm only. If the opponent has not read this manual, he may have your weapon hand as a marker for his distance[1]... And he thinks we have entered into his direct touch zone. A boon for us who did not move our legs (and are therefore at the same distance - out of direct touch reach). At this point all that remains is to punish this mistake with a touch.

---

[1] The poor soul

Do not forget that forward preparations are always done point first with short advances with the legs. Making a preparation with too much forward movement by the legs brings more risks than opportunities:

- You risk going too far into your opponents direct hit zone;
- You risk getting stuck on your legs without being able to get out quickly;
- You risk becoming unbalanced and won't be able to move forwards or backwards (reduction in mechanical possibility).

If we get our opponent to attack and he still hits us, then it is:

- that we are too close;
- that our preparation is too big/obvious;
- that our preparation is too long (in duration), we get stuck;
- that our reaction to the opponent's attack is not right because he caught us by surprise (pay attention to lucidity).

---

## MAKE REACT

All preparations have as a goal to "make react" and, granted, "make act" is already a reaction. But I differentiate between these two intentions in terms of attitude because they don't involve the same continuation of action.

Here our preparation has as true purpose to observe the reaction of the opponent to "the start of an action" with the goal of reconnoitering his intentions and reflexes. Does a prise de fer set him off? By attacking into the attack? Does he retreat out of distance? One must get him to extend his arm or to get him to move his point (to make him change lines = open up his game).

# CONSTRUCTING OUR ACTIONS

As we are prepared, and if our preparation is not too big, we can create an attack in several ways to induce the concept of "second intention".

Let's see how to proceed with our preparations[1] from 3 possible reactions by our opponent.

## IF HE LOOKS FOR THE BLADE

If the opponent has a tendency to try to parry the threat, then we have the opportunity to:

- Continue the action with an attack by disengaging the closed line;
- Keep the tip near the opponent's hand to score when he moves it forward;
- Do not respond immediately so as to drown the fish and wait to for a more opportune time or a larger mistake.

## IF HE ATTACKS INTO THE PREPARATION

If the opponent tends to counter the threat, we can then:

- Parry his attack;
- Create a counter-time in the attack;
- Make his attack fall short :
  - And attacking after our retreat, on his back to "en garde" position;
  - Or not attacking to drown the fish.

---

[1] All of these solutions are only possible if our preparations are controlled, at the right distance, without too much engagement and threatening with the point.

If the opponent tends to avoid the threat by retreating, then we have the opportunity to:

- Push him back to his end of the piste before starting a scoring action (or forcing him to attack);
- Do not follow to drown the fish.

## SCORE A TOUCH

Moving forward to touch is to know in advance that we have deciphered the opponent's reactions and that we have formulated a path to success.

It's starting with foreknowledge based on the analysis of openings observed in the construction of the action.

The intention of touching is not necessarily born by a technical action (lunge or flèche), it can be masked by feigned movements. We must keep in mind that the intention is to score a touch and not the performance of a technical movement!

**The touch is the result of careful construction.** Theoretically, during more than thirty seconds:

- we have observed our opponent's reaction to our feints;
- we have worked the opponent by moving in and out of his direct hit zone;
- we have worn him down (mentally or physically) by feinting, by threatening, or by distracting his attention (on our hand, on our blade).

We are always lucid, him less. We can then decide to bring the action that will deceive him and score a touch.

When we move forward to make act or make react, we are prepared to observe and react as needed. As we are prepared and balanced in proper en garde, we can respond in different ways during the exchange by taking advantage of opportunities or varying our reactions to drown the fish.

Before starting a scoring action, it is appropriate to distinguish between true and false signals. To distinguish between those voluntarily given by the opponent or those caused by our preparations.

When moving forward to touch, do not stop "to see." Continue to the end of the action to finish the hit. It is a voluntary decision taken after gauging the opponent's signals in order to anticipate his reactions and reduce uncertainty. At the start of the attack, the mental pattern of implementation of the action already exists in your mind and can thus be performed more quickly.

## THE ADVANTAGE TO THE ONE WHO DECIDES

Remember that, when deciding the action to be taken, the time between making the decision and starting the action is short; it is a sort of action through anticipation to foil the opponent's observed reactions (reflex signals).

This decision making attitude gives a primordial advantage: **determination**. In deciding to go for the touch, we gain a head start on the opponent to allow for remises if the original attack was not the right strategy (or its technical realization was unsatisfactory). Thus, even being caught by a parry, we can have a head start on the riposte with a sharper and more effective reflex for the remise.

To be determined, it is important to **have confidence** in your actions that lead to scoring. Starting an action is to make a decision that we must see through to its end: the touch.

In addition, self-confidence reduces the time for action by the absence of hesitation. And to have confidence in your actions, there is nothing better than having had time to observe your opponent's reactions to your preparations for choosing the right action and the right time.

For even more efficiency in your actions, decide simple actions. These will always be faster in execution and assert more your decision, giving you more confidence for the following actions.

## INCLUDING A PREDETERMINED ACTION (A VARIATION FOR SKEPTICS)

Go into a bout without any other idea other than to apply the principles of the Fantastic 4 (without thinking of a specific "stroke") and build your technical solutions during the exchange in terms of your opponent's reactions.

After observing the opponent's reactions to your preparations, threats, and other invitations, during the exchange, decide on a stroke (the so called "predetermined action").

When the stroke is selected, you must continue working to reach optimal conditions to use it while hiding your intentions. Keep your distance (out of direct reach), choose the right time (when the opponent loses his lucidity) without distraction (do not focus your attention on the hand) and with the right intention (depending on your choice of stroke).

If the right opportunity does not present itself quickly:

- you can wait patiently by continuing to prepare with a view to absolutely use this stroke[1]
- You can change your mind so as to adapt your technical solution to new reactions by your opponent[2]

---

[1] At the risk of losing your attention to other threats or opportunities that arise

[2] At the risk of getting lost in a technical quagmire faced with changing reactions by the opponent...

Be careful, your intention should be to "hit with this stroke," not "use this stroke to hit." This distinction is important because it impacts your attitude and determination that you hold at the start of your attack.


## CHOSING THE RIGHT STROKE

*"How to choose the right stroke?"*

There is no real answer to this question. We all have our own technical capabilities and habits. The goal is to thwart the opponents reactions observed during the bout. There is not one solution for a given situation, depending on the time, preparations, and opponents. Some basic examples would be:

- If he parries: feint to avoid blade;
- If he avoids blade contact: get him to attack to intercept;
- If he intercepts: keep distance;
- If he counter-attacks: make him lengthen to intercept;
- If he stays out of distance: don't attack;
- If he attacks: parry or keep distance...

But the opponent's actions are often not that simple...

Try to keep in mind that if you are parried (or if your attacks fall short) it is not necessarily because the parry was well done. It may be because your attack was not started from the right distance, or at the right time, and with the right intention... It's a matter of perspective[1].

---

[1] Further analysis can be found in the chapter "After Action".

Be aware, in addition to being well set (what I mean is: be in a good en garde position and having good technical execution) and starting with an actual intention of touching, your initially imagined attacks will transform themselves, during their execution.

It is an almost "magical", derived from understanding the science of the blade. An intention to disengage with the point and the hand in the right position can, for example, transform involuntarily into a beat while attacking if it hits the opponent's foible without enveloping it.

This is another reason to be inflexible on your hand position.

*1*

---

[1] French version of MA (Make Act) / MR (Make React) / T (Score a Touch)

Again, there are signals to interpret the lack of intention in our actions.

*If you end up getting hit on an advance (or any other preparation)*

- It is that we were not prepared to respond to the reaction of the opponent. We advanced without intention.
- Or because the advance was too large: distance error.
- Or your "point-leg" coordination was not good. We advance leg first before the point of the weapon creating a "false threat"

*If during the execution of our attack the opponent is retreating*

- We started the attack at the wrong time. This is probably because we had not decided on the launch of the action, he made us attack or he was not surprised at all.

*If our opponent parry-ripostes our attack*

- We did not read our opponent's reactions to our feints (perhaps he hid them well) but then if he was lucid enough to outwit us it is also that we were not patient enough.

In all cases, technical responses should only be reflexes, automatic responses, developed through repetition during lessons. Do not think about them during the bout, otherwise you would limit the possibilities of reactions.

For example, a tennis player doesn't go on the court with the simple idea of scoring with "a cross-court backhand." He constructs his points according to the opponent's returns and choses his strokes depending on opportunities and openings created in the exchange. It's the same on the fencing piste. Make your preparations and stay ready for openings.

Keep in mind that indecision is a mistake. Whatever you do, have a calculated intention.

Here is a brief summary of things to remember: Intentions

1. Make decisions
   - Never do any forward action without knowing the purpose (feint, move, threat, touch...). Indecision is a mistake. Trust your choices.
2. Observe your opponent's reactions
   - Preparations have to be used to observe the opponent's reactions.
3. Be determined
   - Moving forward to touch (not to make a technical action) gives the advantage of being committed to the touch and allows you to remise more quickly when needed.

# Chapter 3: Putting into practice

*"Ok, that is great in theory, but... how do I apply it?! I cannot think of all of that all the time!"*

I warned you that it was difficult.

Ultimately, you are not expected to come up with a strategy using the "Fantastics" before starting the bout. This "conceptual classification" should not replace your instincts. What I hope with the issues raised here is to help you sharpen those instincts to exploit the best possibilities of scoring a touch, in an intuitive and natural way. It is normal that implementing a new method of fencing epee would need to be done in a conscious way but, with a little work and luck, it will gradually become second nature.

To do this, we must work as rigorously as possible on the fundamentals and technical skills. They must become so automatic that their execution does not draw on your mental resources (concentration).

It's the same for the "Fantastic 4". Through rigorous training, we absorb those things which become an integral part of our game.

You see, it's about being focused and not doing just anything, at any time. The key words are: <u>rigor</u> and <u>mastery</u>!

- Be in a proper en garde position;
- Focus on the target with peripheral attention;
- Master your forward actions;
- Play with the distance to threaten;
- Without forgetting the ultimate goal: to score a touch!

The advantage of this method lies also in the fact that there are only 4 things to integrate[1]. <u>Just construct your touches by varying the game</u> with these points in mind:

- Vary the threats (target);
- Vary the distances;
- Vary the intensities (patience);
- Vary the intentions.


The Fantastic 4s qualify as a method for good epee fencing. If you master them you will be able to construct each match in an optimal way. They are not a series of steps to undertake but a mindset to be used with during the action and its analysis.

Whatever your technical abilities, fencing epee comes back to trying to touch without being touched. This is an objective involving a physical and mental investment to manipulate the opponent and make decisions each of which can be assessed on the basis of the Fantastic 4.

→ Focus on the Fantastic 4 to manipulate the opponent.

---

[1] I even added different coloured logos as a mnemonic device.

# I. MANIPULATION

The goal of combat sports is to manipulate the opponent! How to do that fencing epee?

It is about trying to control the power struggle which establishes permanently between two opposed adversaries.

- By conditioning the opponent through false reactions;
- By surprising the enemy through changes in rhythm or target;
- By marking his mind with a good hit, then using the same action to threaten him to which he will react.

## CONDITIONING

*"How to condition the opponent?"*

By accustoming him, during the bout, to a reaction. We will be able to:

- imprint a constant rhythm;
- repeat footwork patterns;
- threaten using conscious and obvious actions...

Make everything obvious so that, once you notice that the opponent is starting an action based on these fake mistakes, we can surprise him by responding differently.

Here are some examples of diversions:

- During the bout, try to take the opponents blade several times. When you see that the enemy is anticipating (he tries to avoid my blade or threatens your offering of "open" lines), it's time to attack straight to the body in order to surprise him. With this type of preparation, we can lower our opponent's focus **by giving him false information about our intentions** (diversion).

- During the bout, make your footwork predictable and regular. Once you see that the opponent is following your pattern you can replace a retreat with a quick step forward (change of rhythm) to surprise him by closing distance. With this rhythm, you manage **to lower his attention by accustoming him to a 'slow' tempo**.
- During the bout, when the opponent makes a preparation, react voluntarily by attempting to take the parry. When we see that he is ready to start an attack by trying to avoid the parry, it is all over. What to do?
  a. attack the attack
  b. make his attack fall short
  c. change the direction of your parry

These three options (a, b or c) are good. Note that if you are able to do all three it means that you are more lucid and patient than your opponent (this brings us back to the Fantastic 4).


## THE EFFECT OF SURPRISE

In the finals, if the entire exchange is fenced at a high intensity, based on a single action, you lose all hope of contrast or of surprise. No constant intensity level is likely to work for an exchange or a whole match. **It is the variation between the Fantastic 4 that creates real actions that surprise opponents.** As said before:

- Vary the threats (target);
- Vary the distances;
- Vary the intensities (patience);
- Vary the intentions.

All this for the sole purpose of misleading/manipulating/fooling the opponent (call it what you will), to get him to fall prey to your strengths.

Controlling the power struggle is to decide when you and your opponent engage. Decide by imposing the start of the action and varying your hit actions to surprise the opponent (with explosiveness...why not?).

Thus, touch after touch, doubt and indecision settle into the opponent's game.

## INTIMIDATING

Building a game through intimidation is only possible after scoring a touch "that hurts" (not physically but mentally).

Intimidate your opponent by successfully placing a nice touch to the hand, foot, back, on the target (but with 3 kilos[1])... just to rattle your opponent and follow this with successive hits born from faking the repeat of the first hit.

- After a foot touch = fake to the foot.
- After a coupé to the outside of the hand = fake others.

If the touch has effectively rattled your opponent, reactions to future feints will be all the greater (and therefore with larger and more obvious errors). Then we must build upon this base— forward and always with intention.

When you find yourself on the other side of this fence, having taken this kind of "nice hit" be careful not to fall into the trap. Do not panic, analyze your mistake by referring to the Fantastic 4 and do not reproduce the same error (see chapter "After Action").

---

[1] An expression meaning that was touch was "significant".

Here is a brief summary of things to remember: Manipulation

1. Win the power struggle
   - Win the power struggle through cunning and calculated attitudes.
2. Control your opponent
   - Condition the opponent to a rhythm (or a type of preparation) to surprise him by changing it at the start of the scoring action.
   - Successfully score a significant hit and then use the same action in the following exchanges as a fake.

# 2. CONCENTRATION

The application of the Fantastic Four method, and fencing epee in general, requires a significant amount of concentration. The mind is often overlooked in favor of more technical considerations. Here I will try to convince you of the importance of the mind.

What kind of concentration do we need before, during, and after an exchange?

Here are some examples for these three phases with my vision of possible strategies/reactions.

## BEFORE ACTION: STRATEGY

Let's look at a situation.

The match is about to start. No matter who we are fencing it is the same. We must focus on the Fantastic 4 and keep in mind what each means:

- Focus on the target
  - don't follow the hand
- Distance
  - stay out of direct touch distance
  - impose the distance of the fight
- Patience
  - consciously decide the start of the scoring action
  - do not start the action until you have lowered the opponent's concentration.
- No forward action without intention
  - make act
  - make react
  - score a touch

You can add one or two basic reminders, depending on your habits. For example, for me:

- Keep the proper en garde position (point in line and back leg well flexed)
- Fence to win (we aren't just having fun, this remains a fight with one winner in the end—and it might as well be us)

These points are enough. **Do not add technical considerations** ("specific strokes") in the preparation of your game. We cannot anticipate the reactions of the opponent to our threats.

We cannot build an entire game based on physical or technical superiority. At a certain level of competition, all fencers have high physical and technical backgrounds. So we must be stronger than them tactically and mentally.

In addition, think about each game as a different story. Even though you have already fenced an opponent in the past and have found scoring opportunities, know how to manipulate, etc. do not start any new match against him in the same way. You may want to replicate the actions that previously worked but these solutions are from a previous match. To do so we would have to reproduce the conditions in the new game also. This is not always possible. Therefore, constantly question yourself and build scoring actions from scratch[1].

---

[1] Even with the fencers that we know well because we train with them every day.

### > Assess strengths. Understand weaknesses. Whose?

- Yours first, through introspection or analysis with your fencing coach, from training to analyze your overall capacity and improve your weaknesses.
- Your opponent next, to know how to adjust your game when fencing. With passive observation of your opponents you will know what to focus on or be wary of in order to be best prepared during your match.

In training you can work on you strengths or weaknesses. There are no cutting corners here; the idea is to be good on all fronts[1]. Failing to do this, know your strengths so that, during a match, you can steer your opponent to them and have the upper hand in the power struggle.

## CREATE A "FANTASTIC 4 FORM[2]"

Here I am introducing new concepts to help with pre-match analysis. Questions that I (and in the Fantastic 4 method) believe are important to systematically ask to be best prepared.

Here is a method to analyze any fencer's strengths and weaknesses through self-analysis or from observation. I have included a form to help you in assessing important points about a fencer (you or your opponent's). Although this is optional it is a great learning tool to practice observing the important elements of the Fantastic 4 method.

---

[1] This takes time for everyone, unfortunately.
[2] You can find blank copies (PDF) for you, your students, and your opponents at www.howtofenceepee.com.

Here we aren't looking at elements such as "Does he use a French grip or a pistol grip?" rather let us focus on the really important points:

General Information

- Height/speed/explosiveness → To adjust distance;

For example, against a smaller but faster fencer than you, you will have to maintain greater distance. The speed of his attacks lengthens the zone of direct touch.

- The hand game → To adjust our en garde positions on the piste;

Depending on the opponent's hand game we will know how to place ourselves and adapt our position to negate his game plan.

- The kind of strategy → To adjust our attitude.

Offensive? Defensive? Counter-offensive? Complete? Combative? Direct attacks? Combination attacks? ... Here are some factors to observe during the match that require adjustment in strategy.

These points are scored from "not at all" to "a lot". For some of them it is possible to note "Somewhat" if the characteristic exists but is not really marked.

Legend
○ Not at all   ◑ A bit   ● A lot

## Application of the Fantastic Four

Here, we look to see how the adversary applies the Fantastic 4 (even unconsciously) to discover what we can do to take the upper hand in the power struggle.

- Focus on the target;
- Mastery of distance;
- Patience;
- Intentions of actions.

These points are marked with 5 stars for a little more precision. Thus, you can more accurately assess the differences between your opponents or your own progress with each Fantastic. It is also possible to add comments as well.

All these points are not always easy to observe accurately[1]. So take precautions regarding your analysis before the match. Formulate your strategy in broad terms, and test it during the first third of the match.

➔ Before reading "What to do with this analysis", find an example (mine) on the next page.


## WHAT TO DO WITH THIS ANALYSIS?

This form allows you to gain perspective on strengths and weaknesses at a given time. The requirement of maintaining discipline, the irregularity of our fitness, mood swings, nutrition, sleep patterns, training phases, rest... all these factors affect your body (your energy capacity). This makes any analysis subject to change.

---

[1] Especially since a fencer you are analysing can be currently adapting him game to his opponent of the moment.

# General informations

First name : Clément
Last name : Schrepfer

**Legend**
○ Not at all  ◐ A bit  ● A lot

○ Small      ○ Medium    ● Tall
● Slow       ○ Fast      ◐ Explosive

○ Left handed  ● Right handed
● Leads with the point      ◐ Looks for the blade

○ Defensive   ○ Offensive   ● Complete
● Attacks forwards targets   ○ Direct actions
◐ Impose rhythm              ◐ Combative

# The Fantastic Four

### Target
★★★☆☆

Be carefull not to follow the hand

### Distance
★★★☆☆

Profit more from my height

### Patience
★★☆☆☆

Force myself to be more patient

### Intentions
MA ★★★☆☆
MR ★★★★☆
T  ★★☆☆☆

Make act, OK

Make react, OK

Don't forget to touch...

How to fence **Epee**
The fantastic 4 Method

Therefore regular analysis of where you are at in terms of the Fantastic 4 is necessary. Develop the reflex of continual self-analysis when practicing - repeat, repeat, repeat!

You can add general comments about your present state on the day of a competition. For example, once finished your warm-up, reflect on your strengths and weaknesses at present—ask yourself whether your usual strengths are there. You can also focus on your weaknesses to mitigate them.

## GAUGING THE POWER STRUGGLE

From the perspective of a confrontation, this form can also help you to gauge the power struggle that awaits you. With the assumption that you have already seen your opponent's game, try comparing your strengths and weaknesses to define a tactical plan before starting the game.

Every difference is an opportunity to create an adjustment to the power relationship (positive or negative) and can be anticipated before the match. The more positives in your favour, the more you can use these aspects of the game to turn the tide to your advantage. If the power struggle is in the opponent's favour, you must be careful not to fall too easily into his traps.

For example:

|  | Me | The Opponent |
|---|---|---|
| | Tall | Medium |
| | Slow/a bit explosive | Fast/Explosive |

| | | |
|---|---|---|
| **[hand icon]** | Right handed | Left handed |
| | Moves the point well /looks to take the blade somewhat | Takes the blade a lot |
| **[dice icon]** | Complete game | Defensive game |
| | Attacks forward targets | Direct attacks |
| | Can control pace of game/not overly combative | No rhythm/ very combative |
| **[arrow to target icon]** | ★★★☆☆ | ★☆☆☆☆ |
| | Doesn't follow the hand | Follows the hand |
| **[double arrow icon]** | ★★★☆☆ | ★★★☆☆ |
| | Controls distance well | Controls distance well |
| **[arrow to body icon]** | ★★☆☆☆ | ★★★★☆ |
| | Not patient enough | Very patient |
| **[triple arrow icon]** | ★★★☆☆ ★★★★☆ ★★☆☆☆ | ★★★★☆ ★★☆☆☆ ★★★★☆ |
| | Makes react | Makes act |
| | Lacks conviction when attempting scoring touch | Determined when attempting scoring touch |

This table shows the differences that can be observed before the match. From this you can find spots where you can gain advantage over your opponent.

Comparing the data:

- I can already see tactical solutions to implement in a winning strategy:
  - He follows the hand, he looks to take the blade too much, and he is not strong on the attack → the objective would be to get him to attack, or to react by preparing to the hand to score with a second intention.
- I know where I need to be careful:
  - He is fast, patient, and combative → I will have to pay attention to distance, not to rush, and fight hard for each point.

The game looks pretty tight; each opponent has strengths to assert that may give advantage. The fencers' abilities are different and the power struggle is going to be necessarily linked to these differences. Thanks to this, we design a tactical strategy before the bout, which is already an advantage - we have a game plan. It remains to apply the strategy during the bout.

## DURING THE BOUT: OBSERVA(C)TION

We have our action plan and the referee says "Allez." There is no procrastinating, the goal is to touch. Don't rush, gauge distance while concentrating on the opponent's target. Then, each forward movement must have intention, as indicated by this fencing method.

Pay particular attention to each advance in order to never be surprised by the opponent's reactions. Or even if surprised, we have been prepared to respond after our preparation by mental anticipation.

## IF THE MATCH DOESN'T GO AS EXPECTED?

What if the opponent refuses to play, to take part in the exchange, to react to my feints?

### IF HE DOESN'T REACT TO YOUR FEINTS

He may be too lucid to fall for your traps. But, you must continue to press without giving up. That is to say, control the distance while allowing yourself for moments of relaxation by backing out of distance; "backing off" from applying pressure because it does not wears out (physically) the opponent only.

Beware, this does not mean that we exaggerate our feints as we can be punished by making silly distance mistakes (large steps) or hand mistakes (by exaggerating the opening lines in our preparations). Be patient and rigorous - solutions will emerge.

### IF HE DOESN'T PLAY WITH DISTANCE

If you are surprised by your opponent's attacks, he is still too close and you don't have time to apply your game plan.

This is because he refuses to follow your pace and doesn't maintain the fencing distance you are trying to impose (or that he does not react to your threats preparations). He attacks at every opportunity and "steamrolls over you." As the exchanges do not last long you must be especially vigilant with your distance since he moves into direct touch reach without warning. He attacks directly, with no real preparation and scores...[1] We must succeed in halting this game plan and control the bout and impose "real" fencing.

---

[1] Note to self: do not get annoyed, he has the right to do whatever he wants if he can't find other solutions...

The opponent does not keep the pace I impose, and refuses to fight.

He must be encouraged to participate in the exchange by making him move his hand, impose your pace and maintain control of distance to exhaust him mentally. All these provocations (invitations, false errors from the hand or by distance, etc.) it causes him to drop his guard mentally. He will start an unplanned action and you will be able to score.

## CREATE AN "ALGORITHM" FOR TOUCHES

During the match, after a few touches, we can determine our opponent's initial reactions and mistakes. One can thus build solutions based on our observations and develop a kind of "algorithm" for scoring:

- If our opponent always reacts in the same way to a specific threat:
  - I can continue thus
- If no,
  - I can have this other reaction

And so on...

Be careful though not to lock yourself into thinking that this algorithm can create solutions in terms of "strokes", that are often too complicated, moving you away from the simpler and open logic of the Fantastic 4.

Remember that solutions must be found during the preparation phases leading to scoring touches by observing the opponent's reactions. The decision as to which scoring actions to be used then flows directly from the preparatory phase, hence the term "Observa(c)tion[1]".

1. we observe
2. then we act

Your actions should be simple to allow fast to execution. They must not become a Gordian Knot. In this area, consider simplicity as the key to success.

*SOMETHING EXTRA*

**How do you handle very specific fencing styles ?**

*The opponent is offensive minded*

If he is strong on the attack and using opposition, we can assume that he is not comfortable defensively. Dominate him by being more offensive minded. By attacking directly or by counter-time (attack in the attack), you should stop his offensive game and move to a domain more suited to yourself (or at least, less suitable to him).

*The opponent is defensive minded*

If he is strong on defence and using opposition, we can assume that he is not comfortable attacking. Force him to end up in the area he controls less and be patient. If he still does not attack, then the game will comes down to getting him to react (by arm extension) to be able to, through counter-time, score a touch.

*YOU have a style characterized as offensive or defensive*

The best solution for you is to try to vary the attitude of the game to surprise your opponents.

---

[1] Two phases so linked as to form one word.

In that way we can develop a defensive mindset on the opponent's side of the piste and an offensive mindset on our own. The difference in attitude doesn't allow the opponent to develop a tactical plan. Leave him uncertain as to how to adapt to the variety of your fencing attitudes on the piste.

During the action, the objective is: **to create surprise,** or at least an opportunity.

Surprise the opponent into believing (feinting) we are making mistakes and attack when the opponent does not expect it (punish a mistake he makes). By being patient in the construction and observation of your opponent's reactions until you have committed to the start of your decisive scoring action.

## PRIORITY TO "THOSE WHO DARE"

In high level fencing, where athletes are physically, technically and mentally superior, the difference will tip in favor of "those who dare." Those who look for the hit with a little more daring and panache, to surprise their opponents, always.

→ Dare to decide to surprise

## AFTER ACTION: ANALYSIS

After each touch during the match, it is possible to step back and analyze what just happened. This is essential to reduce errors, touch by touch, by understanding the opponent's intentions and develop solutions to eventually take over the power struggle.

Here is a little ritual to begin each new exchange in the best mental conditions and build your match in the best way. All in all, it's a matter of 3 to 5 seconds maximum. Nobody will be aware!

*From my own head:*

I have been hit...

> *"Darn[1]! Well, what just happened? Oh yes, I finished the action just standing there stuck on my unbended legs = I'm following his hand too much. Okay, let's go: Distance, Patience, Focus on the target, No forward action without intention. Ready!"*

I have just made a nice touch...

> *"Yes! He fell for that one, on the prep'! Well, "not easy", it was the construction of the hit that made his attack fall short; keep the good preparation work: Distance, Patience, Focus on the target, No forward action without intention. Ready!"*

This is what happens in my head between the hits. It can be broken down as follows:

1.  I feel an emotion (ex 1: a little annoyed; ex 2: happy);
2.  I stop the emotion (the touch is over; I can't redo it);
3.  I analyze (ex 1: problem - which Fantastic 4 did I not do right?; ex 2: warning - the touch was beautiful but it is thanks to the preparatory work);
4.  I refocus on the Fantastic 4 to find the origin of this particular error;
5.  Let's go!

I admit, stopping the emotion is sometimes very difficult. It is easier to get carried away by it. Understand, however, that the impulse (or not) is a matter of choice. See for yourself. Keeping in mind the unique goal of the match (victory) and considering that anger disrupts our concentration, making the choice to win

---

[1] To be polite...

means to stay focused and not get carried away. We must find a way to stop emotion. Feel the emotion, be it positive or negative, then control it before moving on.

## UNDERSTANDING WHERE THE ERROR CAME FROM

I also put the emphasis on the **analysis of the touch**, which for me is a key point in the scoring construction phase of the match. Depending on who scored, there are reactions to have.

### IF WE SCORE A TOUCH

Analyzing the action when you score is as important as when scored upon; know what worked to continue in this direction, and be conscious about how to deviate his attention from this:

- Analyze the opponent's mistake;
- Understand the conditions that allowed the hit.

When we touch, we often focus on the final action that has allowed us to touch. Forgetting so quickly that it took construction over time to achieve the goal.

A touch is the result of a situation built during the exchange. Make a habit of analyzing the situation (and not the hit) when you touch. With this analysis, you can better understand the actions that led up to the hit and reproduce the conditions later in the game.

Have the same reflex. Analyze the situation through the Fantastic 4 without focusing on technical execution. To do this, one must know the signals which allow us to understand the errors. Here are a few.

## Mistakes in the Fundamentals

Some common mistakes of the basics with interpretations:

- having the hand too low (finishing actions with a low hand) → I must bend my back leg
- hit on the hand → I am too close or my hand was not in the right position.
- collapsing in the lunge → I have to hold my torso vertical (and therefore "tighten the glutes[1]")
- I fence without really focusing on scoring → question yourself: what am I doing on the piste?

## Concentration Mistakes

Some common mistakes in concentration on the target with interpretations:

- movements of the weapon's point are too large → I am focused too much on the hand
- legs are not bent enough → I am concentrating too much on the hand
- distance mistakes → I judged my distance based on the hand, this isn't good
- reacting too much to opponent's feints → I am following his hand too much, paying too much attention to threats

## Distance Mistakes

Some common distance mistakes with interpretations:

- being hit on a close target (foot, hand, or thight) → I am too close

---

[1] Pelvic tilt

- make act and still getting hit → I am too close
- attack but fall short → I am too far away

## Patience Mistakes

Some common patience mistakes with interpretations:

- starting scoring actions too quickly → the touch lasted less than 30 seconds
- having your actions countered → the opponent is still too lucid
- not knowing what happened → loss of lucidity
- action started in the middle of the piste → this leaves too many reaction possibilities for the opponent

## Intentions Mistakes

Some common distance mistakes with intentions:

- being hit while advancing → stepping too large, having no intention, or being too close
- taking too many steps → moving without purpose and/or without threatening with the point is taking risks
- attacking without really having the intention of hitting → starting an attack means being determined to score, if you aren't you shouldn't attack

As if that was not complicated enough, all these errors can be linked and dependent on one another.

- Realizing that you did something after you have done it… (therefore, without intention) and at the same time realize that we did not focus on the target, and attacked out of distance. All this happens when one loses lucidity. *Mamma Mia*, it is all there!

## *SOMETHING EXTRA*

The analysis phase is for stepping back from the action that resulted in a hit and ensure you do not repeat mistakes. Here are the questions that you must ask during the analysis phase to understand what domain the error came from (whether yours or your opponent's).

### The Fundamentals

· Was I in proper en garde? Did I lunge properly? Was my torso erect? Were my hips balanced?

· Was I vertical? Knees well bent?

· Where was my point? And my hand?

### The Target

· Where was I looking?

· Did I move my hand too much?

· Was I stuck on my legs?

### Distance

· Was I really at the proper distance?

· Was I too far away? To close?

· Was I too much in the middle of the piste?

### Patience

· Was I lucid? Do I know what happened?

· Did I wait long enough for my opponent's mistake?

· Was I ready for my opponent's mistakes?

· Did I attack by choice? At the right moment?

### Intentions

· Did I really move forward with intention?

· Was I moving? Was I in preparation?

Knowing how to analyze hits allows you to find solutions for every opponent.

## → WHAT TO REMEMBER

Here is a brief summary of things to remember: Concentration

1. Commit with an open mind
   - Do not engage in thinking about an exchange in terms of technical solutions.
2. Be rigorous
   - Be rigorous with your attention on the game and your opponent's reactions by acting only by choice, building on the fundamentals and the Fantastic 4.
3. Analysis
   - Analyze each hit through the lens of the Fantastic 4 to gradually reduce errors and find areas for improvement.

# 3. MANAGING MATCHES

Here we will talk about the management of the score and time during a game. These two regulatory aspects can induce behavioral changes and influence the strategy and how to implement the Fantastic 4.

## 3 PERIODS = 3 PHASES OF THE GAME

Wherever possible, we must not take into account the score. Staying focused on the Fantastic 4 is the priority. Then, tactically, there are phases to a match, divided into thirds, for which one can adopt good attitudes, outlined in 3 phases of the game:

- The first third time:

The objective is to prepare, work, and observe openings giving the least possible information to our instinctive reactions. Focused and rigorous for 3 minutes, until approximately 5 hits (a sign of patience in building touches).

- The second third time:

The aim is to exploit the openings observed in the first time period. One can increase the physical intensity, be more frank in our intention to hit, especially in our choices of hits. Up to 12 touches.

- The last third time:

The goal is to complete the game by getting the last 3 touches. Building on the actions that worked the best, always focused on distance, patience, and intentions.

Of course, all games are different and the case described above is a case where everything happens "normally" and without a hitch.

Let's now look at some less theoretical cases with more concrete situations, constrained by time.

**Time is a very important parameter in a game.** It can be a decisive factor. Sometimes ally, sometimes enemy, you have to take it into account in the construction of your matches.

 *SOMETHING EXTRA*

### During the break

At the break, you have a minute to catch your breath and your mind. Take the opportunity to reflect on the last 3 minutes. Ask yourself the right questions:

• What has been the winning attitude so far? When you attack or when you defend?
• Where did the hits land? On the opponent's side of the piste, on your side, or in the middle?
• Who was dominating? Who managed to create favourable conditions for scoring?
• Should you continue the strategy? Your strategy works but you must think about drowning the fish so the opponent doesn't notice.
• If no, should you change strategies? What is he doing that bothers you?

These issues need to cross your mind. With or without the help of your coach, you must be able to address these issues without considering technical strokes. Responses should be on the general strategy to adopt. As such you continue to build your strategy effectively during the break.

## A CLOSE MATCH: BE RIGOROUS

When an advantage is difficult to create, we must persevere to find the weakness, analyze errors and strengths of both sides. Try to vary lateral lines, vary intentions, distance, pace, and above all: remain lucid to continue to wear out the opponent.

In a case where each opponent takes turns hitting or there are repeated double touches, we must think about taking time to change strategies and find the loopholes that will finally make the difference.

## YOU ARE BEHIND: STICK TO IT

We have not found the solution yet. The enemy seems stronger than us in all areas. We must hang on and try to quietly claw back touches. Refocus on past touches, analyze them and try to change things to destabilize the opponent.

Vary the intensity in one of the following domains:

- laterally,
- intention,
- distance,
- rhythm ...

And "dare", with more intention of touching, by jumping more audaciously on opportunities for scoring.

But most of all (and still) remain lucid and patient to continue to wear down the opponent (and don't get too worked up).

When things are going too fast and not in our way, we must succeed in delaying the match. We must prolong the exchanges to last about a minute each (watch out for non-combativity rules). As such, at worst, if we are the one who is hit, we would only fall behind by 3 points in a three minute period.

In this case, time is against us. We don't necessarily have the time to develop our touches as we should. It is therefore necessary to "force" the opponent to make a mistake, while using the principles of the Fantastic 4 but adopting a more "daring" attitude to seize opportunities.

## YOU ARE LEADING: STICK TO YOUR GUNS

Don't relax your guard because you are in the lead. It might restore confidence to the opponent by allowing "easy" hits. Why relax and prolong the match? Rather stick to your guns and relax when it's over, right?!

One can imagine that if we are in the lead it is because we have a better strategy than our opponent. You must continue to apply it without wavering until the end of the match. It is useless to survive a close game or make the opponent believe that a winning solution is not far away when it is not.

In this case, time is on your side. So you have everything to gain by taking your time. The opponent is behind and is pressed for time. He will grow impatient and start scoring actions faster. Remain patient and vigilant with a view to punish mistakes, keeping the intention of touching rather than drawing out the time, of course.

If your opponent gradually makes a comeback, it means that there is a problem with your game. You need to refocus on your analysis of what happened after each touch. See what the opponent has understood or what went wrong.

Distance, Patience, Target, and Intention are your allies. **Be focused and rigorous about these** and all situations can turn to your advantage.

Even when we think we have chosen the right action, we can still end up with a double touch (or even a single touch for the opponent). This may mean:

- we didn't succeed in surprising the opponent;
- he was still too lucid;
- our attack was poorly executed;
- or he was lucky (it can happen);

But that does not necessarily mean to do exactly the same thing only faster[1]...

We must analyze the hits through the prism of the Fantastic 4 to understand the problem. Perhaps we made a mistake when analysing the opponent's game!

Anyway, I promise you that the solution lies in one of the Fantastic 4.

## → WHAT TO REMEMBER

Here is a brief summary of things to remember: Managing the score and the time

1.  Take your time
    - Regardless of the score, do not take dumb risks to catch up or slow down if you are in the lead.
    - Time is the third player on the piste, you have to make it your ally.

---

[1] It is the young who often make this mistake. I've been there and I now see juniors making this mistake. It is cute.

# And if he knows this trick?

*"And if the opponent knows and applies the fantastic 4?"*

It's true! How to know if he has? What to do? How do you trap someone who knows the traps? How to get past well laid traps?

It is here that the intensity of the battle reaches its climax! The intentions are hidden until the last moment. The exchanges are built. Solutions vary and evolve gradually throughout the exchanges... hang on, it'll be exciting!

## DETECTING SOMEONE USING THE METHOD

One can fairly quickly gauge the opponent's ability to follow the concept of the Fantastic 4 (even if he does this by instinct, without thinking). Early in the fight, observe all parameters:

- Is he following your hand? Does he follow it when you move? (target)
- Does he stay out of direct touch distance? Does he try to control combat distance? (distance)
- Does he fence without reacting or attacking at the first opportunity? (patience)
- Does he move too much? Do his forward movements seem to have purpose? (intention)

If the answers are no, no, yes, yes, yes, no, and yes, then he follows the principles of the Fantastic 4 and there's reason to worry! The task may be daunting to find a weakness.

In fact :

- whatever his preparations, he expects us to react, he watches and he is ready to jump at an opportunity if we open our lines or do not maintain distance;
- whatever our preparations and attempts to destabilize he focuses on the target and ignores our invitations or threats;
- when he starts a scoring action, he attacks with conviction and determination, without being scattered in complicated solutions;
- each of our attempts to control the exchange by our movements is futile as he seems far away and inaccessible, out of reach.

Now you understand, respecting the Fantastic 4 can develop a strong and difficult game to beat. We do not know what to expect since his game is based on observed openings without being stuck on using a particular technique...

You must, nevertheless, **manage to make him falter in one of the Fantastics.**


## THE SECRET TO GAINING ADVANTAGE

Well... apply the Fantastic 4 rigourously, without falling apart so that you can develop the same kind of "solid" and "difficult to disrupt" game.

Then, if you have both mastered the method, the difference should be on the **rigor** and **boldness** in seizing upon scoring opportunities.

Audacity, of course! Create and seize the opportunities. You are facing a worthy opponent, the solution is not going to offered up on a plate. Go after him carefully but with panache. It is the desire to touch that makes the difference[1].

The rigor in the effective implementation of the Fantastic 4 is difficult to maintain. Thus, the ability to stay focused and only attack to score at the appropriate time is an essential element. Patience (mother of all virtues) will therefore also be an ally of choice to make a difference.

With fatigue (of the opponent) comes a lowering of concentration and imprecision. His gestures, movements, and intentions will be less controlled.

If you manage your energy resources well, you can more successfully implement the Fantastic 4 and the fundamentals.

Causing your opponent to lose focus:

- focus on the target while varying the
  - threats
  - invitations
  - Engagements
  - Slow downs (conditioning)
- by varying distances
- by varying intensities
- by varying and masking intentions
- by not forgetting the objective: touch to win.

Then comes the real game of cat and mouse, hard but enjoyable!

Each preparation is an observation tool, each movement hides a trap, and each touch is a pawn on the chessboard of manipulation... Whoever wins this assault will be the one who has managed to hold it together (rigor) and surprise (audacity). The winner would have exploited his determination to better use by more effectively seizing opportunities opened during the fight.

---

[1] Do they not say that luck favors the bold? Shouldn't we make it our ally?

I have happened to come across opponents who seemed to have the same game plan as me. I found myself facing a mirror, stuck by the idea that they would anticipate my every move and that I would not be able to deceive...

But that's probably because I had not yet read this book[1]!

---

[1] ;-)

# Conclusion

So now, no matter the opponent, regardless of his fencing abilities, you must approach the game with the same technical-tactical ideas in mind. Observing your opponent's reactions during the match will help you identify the elements of the Fantastic 4 that you will unwaveringly implement.

Create solutions with your technical vocabulary but remember that grammar rules are the same for everyone! The Fantastic 4 sheds light on the understanding of these rules and mechanisms that make the modern epee a complete, complex and exciting sport.

Consider formulating your strategy by varying threats (looking at the target), imposing distances, varying intensities and intentions (being patient). The solutions will present themselves, seize these opportunities and gradually minimize your mistakes through detailed analysis undertaken after every scoring situation, and you will become "untouchable"[1].

Do not forget that fencing remains a combat sport. The importance of instinct in combat is not negligible. The Fantastic 4 presented here serve to accompany and complement your instinctive reactions, to optimize possibly but never to be replaced. You must come out victorious in your duel and it is probably by not thinking too much that you will succeed.

Embed this knowledge into your game and your mental practice to understand what happens during the match. Apply this method in training and train your mind to use it wisely, without it taking too much mental resource.

---

[1] Beautiful point of view, is it not?

Do not underestimate your opponent and always analyze each touch in terms of strengths, weaknesses, threats, and opportunities[1] that adversity presents. This will allow you to be ready to respond better to the opportunities that arise during the match.

I hope that reading this method will make you want to test it. Or even better, a whole new dimension to your fencing develops. Not only challenging and engaging but also enjoyable, helping you progress in many dimensions of your fencing!

In all ways, we must persevere! Many of these ideas are not easy to implement but they are based on logical thinking and are tested and approved!

Now that you have the method, you can either have results or excuses, but not both.

I encourage you to follow these last two rules:

- Rule # 1: No longer say: "I do not know how to do it."
- Rule # 2: Do it!

It is a challenge to undertake by ignoring the apparent difficulty. These rules have allowed me to write this first book. I hope they will take you far.

Clément SCHREPFER.

---

[1] Coming soon: Volume 2 "Fencing is marketing" ;)

# Acknowledgements

First of all, I would like to thank Noémie, Patrick and Christophe for their time and their critiques, without which this method would not be what it is. **Thank you** to my reviewers: Michael, Antoine and Emma. Their encouragement and feedback allowed me to deepen my argument by pointing out what they misunderstood and where they disagreed with me. Olivier, **thank you** for your meticulous help.

Of course, **thank you** to Laurent for his advice that changed my vision of fencing (he does not know by just how much).

**Thank you** to Magali for her good sporting sense advice.

A big **THANK YOU** to Hugues for accepting to preface this book.

**Thank you** to my successive fencing masters:

- G. Louisiade
- H. Faget
- J-Y Huet
- B. Benon
- M. Faget
- V. Appolaire
- S. Leroy
- A. Philippe

Who each gave me their vision and passion for fencing. I have had great discussions with them. They saw me grow. They are part of me. **THANK YOU**!!! :'-)

**Thank you** to Ania, Georges, and all those who believed in me. Through their enthusiasm, they allowed me to keep going in this project.

Roland, **thank you** for giving me the impetus to write this method to help you improve. And **thank you** to all my training partners with whom I share so much (and without whom I couldn't train)! ;-)

Last but not least, **thank you so much** Brendan, for what you did for this method and me. Your enthusiasm, your patience and your application were the best things that could happened for this project !

# Somethings Extra

# Appendix:"Fantastic 4 Analysis"

## General informations

First name :

Last name :

Legend
○ Not at all  ◐ A bit  ● A lot

○ Small       ○ Medium      ○ Tall
○ Slow        ○ Fast        ○ Explosive

○ Left handed  ○ Right handed
○ Leads with the point        ○ Looks for the blade

○ Defensive   ○ Offensive   ○ Complete
○ Attacks forwards targets    ○ Direct actions
○ Impose rhythm               ○ Combative

## The Fantastic Four

Target
☆ ☆ ☆ ☆ ☆

Distance
☆ ☆ ☆ ☆ ☆

Patience
☆ ☆ ☆ ☆ ☆

Intentions
FP ☆ ☆ ☆ ☆ ☆
FR ☆ ☆ ☆ ☆ ☆
T ☆ ☆ ☆ ☆ ☆

How to fence Epee
The fantastic 4 Method

Find more the information on

www.howtofenceepee.com

CPSIA information can be obtained
at www.ICGtesting.com
Printed in the USA
BVHW042348220222
629775BV00013B/1544